A SPIRITUAL WORKER'S SPELL BOOK

A SPIRITUAL WORKER'S SPELL BOOK

Draja Mickaharic

Copyright © 2002 by Draja Mickaharic.
ISBN: Softcover   1-4010-8439-7

All rights reserved. No part of this book may be reproduced or transmitted in any form or by any means, electronic or mechanical, including photocopying, recording, or by any information storage and retrieval system, without permission in writing from the copyright owner.

This book was printed in the United States of America.

To order additional copies of this book, contact:
Xlibris Corporation
1-888-795-4274
www.Xlibris.com
Orders@Xlibris.com
17212

CONTENTS

Introduction 9
Chapter One
    Spells Dealing With Economic Improvement 13
Chapter Two
    Spells Dealing With Work and Employment 27
Chapter Three
    Spells Dealing With Romance and Marriage 36
Chapter Four
    Spells Dealing With
    Obnoxious Or Hateful People 56
Chapter Five
    Spells Dealing With The
    Home Or Living Situation 74
Chapter Six
    Charms And Simple Useful Protections 91
Chapter Seven
    Miscellaneous Useful Spells
    Two Spells For Women 98

Dedicated to Helen H.,
Eoghan B., Richard S.,
And especially to the memory of
Major Henry C. Mulburger,
who started it all

INTRODUCTION

Over the course of my many years working with people who have come to me with what they perceive as being problems in their life, I have collected any number of spells and magical techniques of various kinds. Some of these spells require the attention of a person trained in magic to perform satisfactorily. On the other hand, many of these spells are useful for the average person, who can easily use them for their own benefit, whenever the need arises for them to do so. It is these spells, those of general use and utility for the average person, who has had no magical training, which are in this book.

As most of these spells are the kind of useful spell that a spiritual worker would give to someone consulting them, I have called this book 'A Spiritual Worker's Spell Book.' The title is deceptive. Do not think that the use of these spells is limited to those who are professional spiritual practitioners. The truth is quite the opposite. People who find themselves in the negative condition indicated in the book, and who wish to free themselves of the effect of these many different and often difficult negative conditions, may use any of the many useful spells and techniques given in this book for their own benefit.

Not everyone is willing to accept the 'slings and arrows of outrageous fortune,' without fighting back in some way. Those who wish to fulfill a legitimate desire, to return negativity sent to them, or to remedy situations that have challenged their patience, may use any of the spells in this book to good effect.

Some of these spells may seem to be black magic. In fact, any spell that seeks to change the condition in life of any other person, whether for good or ill, may be black magic. The purist will always consider any steps taken to influence another person in any way to be an evil practice, or black magic. Should you consider any of these spells to be either unethical or immoral, please do not use them. There is not ever any requirement that you ever use any spells at all, much less, that you use any spells that you do not approve of.

However, while you have these thoughts, or consider these concerns, please also bear in mind the old military dictum, that the best defense is a good offense. Sometimes a short harsh act directed toward another person can turn away great negativity from coming to rest on your own shoulders. The prevention of difficulty may well justify a harsh act in this event.

Over the course of years, I have seen many spells that seem to require an abundance of rare and exotic materials. Other spells are set in some kind of a formal ritual format, often seeming to require a well-rehearsed cast of dozens, if not thousands. Unlike these more dramatic efforts, all of the spells in this book are to be accomplished with reasonably easily obtainable materials, and are to be performed by the one wishing to do the work themselves. Should any of the materials and other things mentioned in this work be difficult to find, I would suggest that herbal suppliers, botanicas, religious supply stores, and other sources of both religious and spiritual supplies be consulted. Herb and health food stores often have a variety of materials that could be of use in some of these spells, but other more practical sources for the various supplies that may be required should not be overlooked. I purchase the bulk of my candles at a nearby grocery store. This same store also provides me with many of the kitchen cooking spices and other similar ingredients that I use in my practice.

I also understand that there are many sources of supply for occult goods to be found on the Internet. As I am not used to a computer, I do not use the Internet, but those who are familiar with it assure me that it provides a wonderland of information, as well as any number of suppliers of magical materials. I have not listed any sources of supply, and have attempted not to give any complicated spells, or any spells using either exotic or rare materials in this book. At most, people can perform any of these spells alone, although a few using physical manipulation, such as the salt rub, may require the assistance of a friend or a lover.

I do urge you to read the particular spell you intend to use at least twice before attempting to perform it. I have found that most of the difficulty people have had with working these simple spells is caused by their not reading the spell through, and taking the time to thoroughly understand it before trying to work it. Please take the time to learn exactly what you are to do before you begin performing any of these, or any other, spells you might wish to use.

I hope that you find the information given in this small book useful to you in improving your daily life. That goal was my sole intent in writing this book. Your success in using these spells will be my success in making them available to a wider audience.

Draja Mickaharic
New York City, 1998

CHAPTER ONE

Spells Dealing With Economic Improvement

Some Preliminary Considerations

When a person wishes to improve their financial circumstances it is important that they first recognize that there are two factors at work that directly influence their financial status. First, is their own mental conception of their economic place in the world, and secondly there is what the great bounty of the universe can actually make available to them. Once the person seeking money understands the influence of these two factors on their personal financial status, they may open their ability to increase their financial state to greater control and easier manipulation.

Those who believe that they have a right to a great deal more money, and a far higher life style than they presently find themselves in are in the position of actually blocking their economic evolution more effectively than anyone else could possibly do by performing negative magical work against them. Many of these people secretly or sub consciously often believe that they are inferior to others in some way. These people often compensate for this deep and hidden fear of their own inferiority by demanding a more luxurious and elaborate lifestyle than those around them have. So long as the universe is in a period of expansion toward these people, usually in their youth, they may actually attain this preferred lifestyle. Eventually however, the universe begins to contract on them, and their idealized lifestyle eventually settles down to what is actually going to be materially available to them. Often at this time, they are in the position of being dependent on another person for their support in the world, or they may lose the high economic place they may have thought that they attained. Either may be as grating to their internal desires as if they were without any financial support at all.

We must all accept that in our so-called civilized world, money is one of the ways in which the creator of the universe supports and sustains his creation. Therefore, divine law ultimately regulates the flow of money, and the creator apportions it to mankind as the creator desires. Money is always both a test and a temptation in the hands of those who have it. This is especially true in the case of those who have accumulated great wealth, either through effort, inheritance, or by the chance of fate.

The individual must understand principle of the divine origin of money and wealth to grasp the function that money actually plays in the divine scheme of things. When people yield to the temptation of money, they usually find that no matter how much money they have, it will slip through their fingers like water, leaving them with only the burning desire to ever have even more. Eventually, money will no longer come to them as freely as it once did. These people will then find themselves in a very difficult situation indeed. However, the flow of money is always ultimately in the hand of the divine, and it is important to both realize and accept that the creator knows best what to do with money and wealth. Being jealous of a person who has received a sum of money, or even resenting someone who has accumulated a great fortune, is just one more way to block your own path to attaining greater financial resources of your own.

In addition to the mental attitude of the person themselves, there is also a principle in the universe known as the sphere of availability. This principle relates directly to the amount of economic support that the universe is willing to provide any particular individual at any given time in their life. The sphere of availability for each person is variable, in that it may be either expand or contract by the thoughts, actions, and beliefs, of the person themselves. The more sincerely grateful that a person is, and the more truly charitable they are, the greater their sphere of availability becomes.

On the other hand, the more greedy that a person is for material things, and the more they turn from properly relating to their fellow man in a charitable way, the more their sphere of availability contracts. As the personal sphere of availability increases, more financial support becomes available to a person. Contrariwise, as their personal sphere of availability decreases, the person will have made less financial support available to them from the bounty of the universe.

Generosity and charity to our fellow man is actually our duty on this earth, it is not an optional task to be undertaken only when we desire to accept it. True charity is always expressed by the direct donation of our time and attention, as well as both our material goods, our money, and the other necessities of life, directly to those who we perceive to be actually in need. Giving ten million dollars, or any other sum, to any organized charity is simply buying public adulation, a tax deduction, or both. This kind of supposed charity actually has less real spiritual benefit attached to it than giving a dollar to a panhandler. Giving money anonymously to someone in need, without the recipient, or anyone else, being aware that you are the donor, is always something that works directly to your spiritual advantage. Openly or publicly giving sums of money to any person, cause, or organization, is buying the approbation of your fellow man, and in many cases purchasing a deduction from your tax levy.

Making any great show or display of your supposed charity is always a spiritually destructive act. You must not count show or display in your heart or your mind as charity. If you wish to increase your sphere of availability, give small sums anonymously, without any concern at all as to what the recipient does with the money you have given them. Giving quarters and dollars to beggars on the street is actually more spiritually productive than giving large endowments to major public charitable institutions.

Many times an individual will not notice the slow shrinkage of their personal sphere of availability. Later on, a sudden financial downfall may reveal this shrinkage, as in the loss of a paying position, or in a surprising bankruptcy. The same is true of the sudden increase of the sphere of availability, as when winning a substantial lottery prize. The operation of the sphere of availability is not usually noticeable, but its operation in your life is relentless. Your personal sphere of availability is constantly either expanding or contracting, as you change your attitudes and your personal practices over the course of time.

In this regard, monetary greed—the constant desire for more—is always a limiting factor that tends to reduce a person's sphere of availability. The difficulties encountered by displaying monetary greed are one of the best reasons for not repeating money spells, or other work for economic evolution. Even in the most desperate circumstances, the person seeking money must consider their attitude and beliefs. If their attitude toward money is negative, the universe is unlikely to reward them with additional funds. In this case, any spells that the person may cast, or that other people may cast for them, are unlikely to be very successful.

When a person thinks of himself or herself as being 'only a poor student,' or 'living in poverty,' and especially when they believe that they are someone who deserves to receive things either for nothing, or at the lowest possible price, they probably have already severely limited their potential income by their own thoughts. Those who believe that the universe should care for them as they sail through life without doing any work at all are in much the same place. These people have milked their sphere of availability dry, and eventually it will collapse upon them. The collapse may not come until much later in their life, but it will eventually arrive, usually at a time when it will teach the person the harsh and often bitter lesson of their prior poor attitudes toward life.

On the other hand, some people seem to go through an entire lifetime, gliding along without a care in the world. While other people always seem to be struggling hard just to make ends meet, working hard and yet never seeming to be able to keep their heads above water. These people do not provide a demonstration of the inequity of the world, but rather they give a graphic example of how the practices of one lifetime can lead into the quality of another life. Treating whatever money you receive gratefully, as if it were the creator who supplied it to you, and practicing true charity to your fellow man, are ways to avoid this difficulty.

When a person is not doing what they can in the world to earn their own money, it is unlikely that they will find that their prayers, or any other work they do for money will be successful. You must always remember that money is one way in which the creator of the universe supports his creation, but the creator expects you to also do what you can to bring money to yourself. When you look at the idea of performing money spells of any kind to increase your financial status, you should always bear these important facts foremost in your mind.

Money Charms

A General Spell to Improve the Finances of a Home

Note: This spell is only useful for a home. Please do not use this spell for a place of business.

Take about a quarter cup each of dry black beans, dry chickpeas, and dried corn or wheat. Mix them well, and make four packets of the mixture in plain white paper or in plain white cloth packets. Place one packet in each of the corners of the main room of the house, placing three shiny pennies on top of each packet. Leave the packets there for some time, several months or a year is the usual time required. Over this time, the financial condition of the home will slowly improve. This if the money that comes into the home is being well managed this will especially be true.

Using a Nutmeg for Drawing Money

In my book '*Century of Spells*' I mention the 'Gambler's Nutmeg' on page 103. This prepared nutmeg is used to draw money to the person who carries it. Those who have discovered they can make money by gambling especially favor it. The prepared Gamblers nutmeg may be carried in the pocket as a permanent charm if desired. Because of its reputation for drawing money, it is a favorite charm for gamblers to carry on their person while they are playing games of chance.

To make a gamblers nutmeg, take a whole nutmeg, available in the spice section of most grocery stores. Drill a small hole in the stem end, a 1/8-inch diameter hole a half inch or a bit deeper is about right. Clean out the nutmeg shavings, and put a drop of mercury into the hole. Seal the mercury in place with a few drops of red sealing wax or the drippings from a red candle. Anoint the nutmeg with a drop of sandalwood oil, and pray over it that it bring money to yourself, or to the person for whom you have made it. Place the prepared nutmeg into a new charm bag, and you have your money drawing gamblers nutmeg charm.

A plain nutmeg carried in the pocket will do almost as well for many people, although it is not ever recommended for those who use the nutmeg for its money drawing properties when gambling. The prepared gamblers nutmeg is far better for those who have found that they can consistently make money when gambling. These people seldom lose when they gamble.

On the other hand, if you find that you cannot consistently make money gambling, you should avoid gambling altogether. It is not one big win that matters, but the consistent ability to win money at gambling day in and day out. Some people have this rather rare ability while others do not. It is important to recognize on which side of this gambling fence you are actually located. Most people are not able to gamble successfully, even once in a while.

If you find that you cannot make money gambling, you can be assured that the money you require will always come to you in some other way. Allow the universe to supply your needs, and have faith that you will be taken care of. Your task is to do what you can in this direction, 'trusting on the lord' that he will do his part in taking care of you.

As a slight insight into the process of using nutmegs to draw money, I have personally discovered that sprinkling a bit of powdered nutmeg into the bill compartment of a new purse or a new pocket wallet seems to keep the purse or wallet more comfortably full. I recommend this simple spell to you as a good practice to follow. It can certainly do neither you nor your funds any harm, and it even seems to enhance the smell of a new leather billfold.

A Lodestone Money Charm for the Home

Often known as the 'Pot of Gold' money spell, this money charm is one that spiritual practitioners often make up for their clients. The charm is made from two lodestones, natural magnets used magically since antiquity for attracting what is wanted to someone. This is apparently a secret money charm or spell, as far as I know, it has never been written about previously. Nevertheless, it is a very well known spell among most of the spiritual practitioners whom I have met. There are always a number of minor variations in the spell itself, as they are given between spiritual practitioners. This is normal, as no two practitioners do things in exactly the same way. This is how you make this charm, which has successfully helped a great many people.

Two lodestones, one 'male' and the other 'female,' as indicated by their attracting each other and fitting together fairly tightly are to be used. I suggest that the person preparing this charm personally select the two lodestones, as this will give a more successful result than buying them without assuring yourself that they will both attract and fit together. This usually requires a long visit to a botanica or a spiritual supply store, spending time sorting through lodestones. This is still a better choice than buying the lodestones by mail order from an unknown vendor.

The pair of lodestones selected is placed into a bowl, and the following material is added to the bowl:

A teaspoon of iron filings, which are to 'feed' the lodestones.

A few of the gold and silver sprinkles or sparkles found in Botanicas, and sometimes found in paint or art supply stores. A dash of these sprinkles is enough don't overdo these.

Several grains of wheat, or the heads of three stalks of wheat that have the grains of wheat on them.

Some copper, a copper disk or copper coin, like a pre 1980 copper penny, or even better, some copper shavings.

Five dimes. These do not have to be silver dimes.

A few straight pins.

Some grains of dried corn, grains of hard corn or Indian corn are usually preferred.

Something that reflects, like a small mirror from a purse-sized compact or some shiny sequins that can reflect an image.

Three pieces of coral. Red coral is usually considered to be the best, but white coral may also be used.

This assembly is prayed over, either by a spiritual practitioner, or by the person making this charm for himself or herself. The prayer should include the name of the person the charm was made for, and a statement that they should always have sufficient money in their life for the necessities of life, as well as excess for recreation, and taking pleasure in their life, and funds to put away for their old age.

The person receiving this charm is always instructed as to how to use it for their greatest benefit. Firstly, they are always to keep the charm hidden away in a safe place. Under no circumstances is it ever to be viewed by others, or ever even shown to anyone. The person who makes or who is given this charm must take care to feed their lodestone charm only when they are alone. This precaution is necessary because this charm may be destroyed by the unconscious jealousy or envy of another person who might be shown it by the owner. These charms may even be harmed by the unexpressed subconscious envy of a mate.

Secondly, on Tuesdays, the person who the charm was made for is to take the lodestones out of the bowl, and put them into a glass of water that has had a teaspoon or so of whiskey added to it. The stones are to sit in this water for about a half an hour, or so. Then they are to be taken out and prayed over by the person, who asks for what funds they believe they may need in the coming week. The person should always ask for money for food, and whatever other money they may need for the coming week. Asking for an amount slightly greater than will be enough to pay your expected bills is considered a reasonable request. The lodestones are to be replaced in the bowl, and some iron filings, about a quarter-teaspoon full, are added to the bowl. Then the lodestone charm should be hidden away again. The person may drink from the water the lodestones have rested in if they wish. While drinking the water is usually considered a good idea, several other spiritual practitioners do not recommend it. They believe the water should be sprinkled around the house. Other practitioners recommend using whiskey in place of water in feeding the charm. If everything is going well with this charm, the lodestones will very gradually grow in size. This is because the iron filings you have added to them stick and become attached to the lodestones over the passage of time.

A Tip Basket Spell

I once had a girl come to me who worked as a coat checker at a restaurant in Brooklyn. She checked coats in the evening from four until midnight, which was considered a very profitable shift. However, she had found that the amount of money she was receiving was not as great as she had expected to be taking in. She asked me for my assistance in the matter. I happened to have a wicker or raffia basket that had contained some fruit. I took the basket, and making up a large quantity of cinnamon tea in a canning kettle, I put the basket in the tea and let it soak in a simmering heat for several hours. The heat off, I took the basket out and allowed it to dry. Then I prayed over the basket that it might draw money to it. I gave the basket to the girl, who was delighted to see the tip income she received each shift increase substantially.

Cinnamon tea is made using a teaspoon of cinnamon to each cup of water. The cinnamon usually should be added to boiling water and the heat turned off immediately as it is stirred into the water. If you wish to have the tea permeate an object, as I did with the wicker basket, you must put the object into the tea as soon as you have turned off the heat, or even continue the heat at a lower level. You should avoid boiling the tea however, as that is too much heat.

Once the tea solution has reached room temperature, the object, which obviously must be something that will be wet by water, is finished. It should be removed from the tea and set aside to dry. Drying a raffia or wicker basket may take three or four days, even when the basket is placed in bright sunlight.

I have also prepared cotton camisoles for two sisters who were waitresses in a midtown restaurant in this manner. The camisoles were soaked in the cinnamon tea solution until it reached room temperature, and then they were dried. I showed one of the sisters how to do this herself, so they could continue to treat the garments after washing them. Both of the sisters reported increased tip income because of wearing these cinnamon treated camisoles under their starched white uniform blouses.

Money Baths

There are a number of baths that have the effect of telling the universe that the person taking the bath needs to receive more money. Baths being utilized to increase a person's supply of money are just another technique for telling the universe that you need money. No matter which technique you use, it is important that in all of the work you do for money, that you are not concerned about the source of the money that will come to you.

Once you take a money bath, or do any other kind of money spell, you should just allow the universe to bring you the money that you require. The universe is always willing to support those who live in it, but it has any number of ways of providing this support to people. The person asking the universe for increased money supply should not attempt to dictate to the universe just how this increased money supply will come to them. After all, you might just find some lose money lying in the street. Several people have done so in the past.

Money Bath #1

Take a bunch of fresh watercress, and tear it apart into small pieces. Do the same with a bunch of fresh parsley. Place this in a pot containing about two quarts of boiling water. Stir the water in a clockwise direction, and then remove the water from the heat. Now add a tablespoon of honey, stir the mixture, and allow the water in the pot to come to room temperature.

Once the water has reached room temperature, strain out the parsley and watercress from the liquid, and then add this water to a tub bath. Bathe for between six and eight minutes, immersing yourself completely at least five times. While you are in the tub, between immersions, pray sincerely for the money you need, adding into your prayer just why you wish to obtain the money. This bath is particularly useful for obtaining the money required for providing for young children. If you are owed back child support, use this bath first. This bath is always a good start on the process of increasing your finances when an absence of child support money is your difficulty.

Money Bath #2

There is a perfume available in many Botanicas known as Lotion Pompeia, Made in France by L. T. Piver of Paris, it is also sold by mail order through some of the Internet spiritual supply stores. This spell requires a small bottle of this perfume, although I have seen this same spell done with other perfumes such as 'Florida Water,' and one known as 'Kolonia 1800.' All of these prepared perfumes are among those available at most Botanicas, and at many spiritual supply stores. Whichever perfume you decide to use, you will only need a small bottle, so purchase the smallest size bottle of these perfumes you can find.

This bath is to be taken on seven consecutive Fridays. It is made by placing a dozen carnation flowers in a tub of water, and adding about a cap full of the perfume. This is only about half a teaspoon to a teaspoon of perfume, or even less. Once in the tub, you are to scrub yourself thoroughly with the carnations, beginning at your feet and working toward your head. As you do this, pray that you always have sufficient money, with excess funds available to allow you to live comfortably and enjoy life. After you have taken the bath, you should air dry, and then just go about your business. The bath's effect usually begins after the third or fourth week, but you must take the bath for all seven weeks for the best financial effects to begin to occur in your life.

The instructions for taking spiritual baths are quite easy to understand. First of all, you should take an ordinary bath, washing your hair, and removing all of the ordinary physical dirt, and the day's soil from yourself. Then begin with a clean bathtub, filled about half full of lukewarm water. The cooler the water the more effective the bath will be, but you should not use water that is so cold as to give you a chill. Place the bath into the tub, straining it through a strainer if you have made it using herbs or solid spices. Enter the bathtub nude, and immediately immerse yourself in the water. Be sure to immerse your head, including your hair. Remember that you should not use any soap, bath oils, or anything else in a spiritual bath. Just you, the water, and the bath solution, are all that should be in the tub.

Remain in the bath for six to eight minutes, or the time specified in the bath instructions, immersing yourself completely several times in the bath water.

While you are bathing you should pray for the results that you want from the bath. In a money bath, you should pray for a stable income sufficient for your needs, with enough excess to make life as pleasant as possible for you. When the time you are to stay in the bath has elapsed, get out of the tub, but don't dry yourself. You want the bath solution to dry on your body. You can wrap your head in a towel, and put on a bathrobe, but otherwise you should air dry. Now don't bathe or wash your hair for twenty-four hours after you have taken a spiritual bath. That gives any spiritual bath you take the best opportunity to have as strong and positive an effect as it can on you.

CHAPTER TWO

Spells Dealing With Work and Employment

A Word about Working

For most people, their work or employment is the sole source of their income. Regardless of how you earn your living, most people are limited to working for a living, 'earning their bread by the sweat of their brow,' as the saying goes. It would certainly be nice if everyone loved the work they are doing, but unfortunately, that is only rarely the case. Many people, including those who have held their job for many years, are actually indifferent to their work, while quite often they may despise the work they do to earn their living.

You must realize that the attitude that you hold toward working for your living is a very important part of how you are able to attain success in your chosen field of endeavor. If you do not like the work you are doing, you should find some way to get into a better position, another line of work, or to make a change of employment. You must find something that you like better than the work you have found that you dislike. You should really do your best to avoid spending much of your life stuck working in a position or occupation that you really do not like.

Today many people begin their employment careers working at some fast food chain, like McDonald's. Very few people plan on doing this kind of work all of their life. America is a land of opportunity, and if you wish to do so, there are always ways in which you can advance yourself in your occupation. You should always take advantage of the many opportunities that are available to you. It is actually your responsibility to do what you can to advance yourself, both economically and professionally, in your chosen field of endeavor.

You must always bear in mind that there are cycles in the universe. All people pass through both good times and bad times over the course of their life. You should take advantage of the good times to lay up as much material benefit for yourself as you can, by saving whatever you can from your income. Then you will find that in the bad times you will not be stranded in any kind of a hard or difficult economic position.

In any job that you may ever hold, regardless of the size of your income, it is important that you always pay yourself first. You pay yourself by saving as much money from your salary as you possibly can.

When you have a job you like, and are working at it, it is important that you take a real interest in your work. Ideally, you should treat your employers business as if it were your own, sincerely performing the tasks assigned you to the best of your ability. In addition, you should always make it a point to arrive at work on time, or even better, a few minutes early. Do not be in too much of a rush to leave at the end of the day either. You should leave with the crowd, not rush to be the first one out of the door.

If you work at an occupation that is covered by a union contract, you should be sure to attend union meetings, and follow the work rules established by the union, whether you agree with them or not. Following these general guidelines will soon convince your employer and your union, if you belong to one, that you are a valuable worker, and one that they should favor. Becoming a valued employee in the eyes of your supervisor or employer will assist you in insuring the stability and permanence of your income at least as much as anything that you might ever be able to do magically.

With the above general rules in mind, several things may be done magically to assist someone in either obtaining or holding a position. One of the most interesting, as well as one of the most effective, is to prepare a magical 'hand' to give you assistance in obtaining a position, as well as assisting you in your daily working life. A 'Hand,' also known as a 'Toby,' is always useful to gain assistance from the universe in obtaining a position, no matter what kind of job you are applying for.

A Hand For Gaining And Holding Work

Begin to make your hand by obtaining one of the red flannel charm bags that are sold in botanicas and spiritual supply stores. If you desire, you may make this bag yourself. Plain red cloth is used. It need not be flannel. Into this charm bag, you should place the following material:

A silver dime—Try a coin store for this, they are known as scrap coins, as you are not concerned whether or not the dime has been circulated, or how worn the coin is. The coin does not have to be anything special, but if you were born before 1964, having a silver coin with your birth year on it is always a worthwhile charm for you.

A piece of cinnamon stick—about a half inch piece of stick cinnamon is all you will need.

Some Cinquefoil herb—Known as Mano Ponderosa, or powerful hand, this herb promotes eloquence and assists you by enhancing your ability to communicate well with others.

A piece of High John the Conqueror or Jalap root. A small piece is all that is required. You will find the herbs and roots you need at Botanicas and spiritual supply stores, as well as in many herb stores. High John the Conqueror root is often sold as a whole nut like piece. You can break or shatter the root with a few hammer blows. This root is to help you overcome any obstacles that may be in your path.

Once you have all of the ingredients in the charm bag, sprinkle the bag with a few drops of rum or whiskey. Then, holding the charm bag in your hands, pray over it for what you wish to have, steady work, a good job that you will like, a better paying position, or whatever else you may reasonably wish to have in the way of work and employment. You should add that the job should provide you sufficient income to live, as well as enough to save, with some excess for pleasure in your life. You should carry this charm with you in your pocket or purse whenever you go out to look for work, as well as keeping it with you while you are employed.

Praying For Day Work

Many people do day work, working by the day from assignments given by a labor brokers or other kinds of temporary employment agencies. If this is the kind of work that you do, you should light a plain white candle the night before you will be calling or visiting the agency you are going to go to for work. Pray that you have work on the following day, and if you wish to work for a specific period of time, add into your prayer just how long you wish to work. Many people have found that praying for work in this way has been very successful for them. It is certainly worth your trying this spell if you need temporary work, or if you regularly earn your living in that way.

Obtaining A Civil Service Position

Many people would like to have a Federal, State, or Local Government, or government Agency, Civil Service position. These jobs are preferred because they are steady, and have good benefits, even though the pay is often lower than is available in the non-governmental job market. In many cases, these jobs take a very long time to obtain from the time you first apply for them until you receive the position. There are a few magical ways of increasing your chances of passing any examination that may be given, as well as increasing your chances of being hired by these different governmental organizations. As with most magic, your sincere prayer actually accomplishes the work.

Let us say that you wish to get a job with the statistical reference section of the Department of Transportation, in their northeast regional office. From the time you are preparing to apply for the job, you should pray each day to the 'Spirit of the Statistical Reference Section of the Department of Transportation, In the Northeast Regional Office.' This kind of prayer may be made because every worldly organization, company, club, association, or governmental agency, has a non-physical or what is generally called a spiritual component, as well as its more obvious physical component. The non-physical component of most of these organizations is almost never recognized by anyone. Like anyone else, the non-physical component of the organization is interested in being recognized by people, especially those who work for it. When this non-physical component is recognized, and asked to help someone join the physical organization, it will usually do its best to do so.

First write out a prayer, similar to the one below, although modified for the particular position you are seeking. Then light a white candle and sincerely pray the prayer each morning, starting as soon as you have decided that this is where you wish to work. Obviously, you should change this prayer to suit the job you wish to obtain, mentioning both the position and the office that you wish to obtain work in with as much detail as possible. The detail of the organization and the information about the position you want in that organization are both important.

An Example Prayer

"I address this prayer to the Spirit of the Statistical Reference Section of the Department of Transportation, In the Northeast Regional Office. Dear spirit, I wish to work in your department as a ____, a position that I know that I am qualified for and can fulfill very well, both to your benefit and to my own. I ask that you assist me in obtaining this position in any way that you are able to do so. I light this candle for you to gain the energy that you may require to be of assistance to me in obtaining this position. I thank you for your assistance in helping me gain work with your organization."

This prayer may also be modified to ask the spirit of the organization to assist you in gaining a promotion in the organization. You may begin making the prayer for promotion once you have been employed in the organization for the necessary length of time to become a permanent or career employee, and you know that a promotion opportunity is actually available for you to fill.

You should always thank the spirit of the organization for the help it has given you. After you obtain either the position or a promotion, you should light at least three white candles, on three successive days, in thanksgiving to the spirit of the organization for the assistance it has given you. When doing this, mention the position you have been employed in, or the promotion you have received, as well as the organization, by name.

It is a good idea to remember that every organization has a non-physical spirit of this kind. You can pray to the spirit of any organization that you wish, and by offering the spirit prayers, praise, and a candle from time to time, you can usually make the organization become more favorably inclined toward you. Those who seek to have power in their church or their community organizations can also use this information to their advantage. As I mention above concerning an employer, it is quite possible to make friends with the spirit of the organization before you decide to join it, or decide to run for an office in the organization.

I am certain that if more people knew about the non-physical components of various organizations there would be more work directed toward them. I have prayed to the non-physical spirit of business organizations to have the organization pay bills owed to my clients. In every case, the organization's non-physical spirit was more than happy to hear from me, and assured me that almost no one ever spoke to it about anything at all. This is true even of the largest corporations, where everyone in the corporation usually woefully neglects the non-physical spirit. If prayed to at all, it is usually prayed to by only a few of the smaller stockholders.

An Examination Spell

This examination spell has a very long record of success in assisting those taking all kinds of examinations, from school examinations and civil service examinations, to professional licensing examinations. I recommend that it be used before you take any kind of examination for a position, such as a civil service test, or even a school or a job placement test. Because this spell has been so often successfully used, I believe that it is one of the few foolproof spells that exist. Obviously, it should only be used if you know that you are reasonably able to pass the test, and are taking a test in a subject with which you have some familiarity. If you have not studied the subject to the point where you are familiar with it, all of the spells in the world will be of no avail to you.

Obtain two orange candles. One candle should be substantially larger than the other is. You are to set the two candles out where you regularly burn candles. The smaller candle is placed into a candleholder and prepared for lighting. The larger candle is laid down next to the smaller candle. Now you make a prayer similar to the following, and then light the smaller candle. Be certain that you allow the smaller candle to burn completely out.

Example Prayer

"I speak to the spirit of examinations, asking your assistance in aiding me to pass the examination for ____. I have studied the material and I am prepared to take the test, but I desire your assistance in taking the test. I light you this small candle to show you of my sincerity in asking for your assistance. When I am notified that I have passed the examination, I will light the large candle that is next to it, in grateful appreciation of your assistance to me in helping me pass this test."

Ideally, you will light the smaller candle a day or two before you take the examination. Then you must wait until you learn the results of the examination, whether you believe that you have passed it or not, before lighting the large candle. Of course, you must be certain that you actually do light the large candle, allowing it to burn completely out, once you find that you have passed the examination.

This spell has been successfully used by several people taking the New York Bar examination, which I have heard is one of the most difficult bar examinations in the country to pass. As I say, this is one of the most foolproof spells that I know of. I am sure that you will find it useful.

Praying Before Working

It is always a good idea to say a prayer before starting to work in the morning. Any prayer you wish may be used, although the Lords Prayer and the 23d Psalm are usually recommended for this purpose. As a part of your prayer, or immediately after it, you should also ask that your trip to work, the time you spend working, and your return trip from work, be both safe and well protected.

CHAPTER THREE

Spells Dealing With Romance and Marriage

Getting and Keeping a Lover

Everyone wants to have a mate or a lover. The desire for someone to share your life with is one of the universal constants of human existence, common among all people, all over the world. As a result, most people devote a good part of their youth to finding a mate, marrying them, and then unfortunately, frequently estranging themselves, divorcing them, or separating from them, later on in life.

These people then usually begin the whole process of seeking the 'right' mate all over again. They do this even without looking into what part they may have played in the failure of their last relationship. Honest self-examination is the key that is needed to having a good relationship. If you really know what you are looking for, and why you want what you are looking for, you will have much better luck in finding a satisfactory mate for yourself.

Before undertaking any spells for romance or marriage, it is important to be certain that the intended couple have the possibility of really being able to form a lasting relationship. It is always very easy for couples to 'wed in haste and repent at leisure.' This is something that is unfortunately very common in the world today.

Before deciding to look for a permanent relationship you should seriously consider whether or not you are temperamentally suited for marriage by carefully looking into yourself. You must begin this self-examination by realizing that not everyone has been destined by the creator for marriage and a family life. If your introspection tells you that you are actually not suited for marriage, you should avoid it, as it will not benefit you.

Do you really look forward to having a family of your own, including having the responsibility for caring for others, dealing with the financial drain of marriage, as well as passing through the many joys and sorrows that having a family brings? If you find that you are not suited for marriage, you may wisely wish to avoid marriage altogether. If you should find that you are not suited for the kind of permanent lifetime commitment that marriage implies, you would probably be far better off remaining single. Quite naturally, it is always much better for you if you discover this before you marry. Once you have married, if you are actually intended to be single, you will go through years of misery, usually ending in the financial and emotional pain of estrangement, separation, and divorce. If you are actually not suited for the married life, the single life will be far better for you.

Permanent alliances aside, there are several sexual attraction spells that may draw a temporary lover to solve the problem of those occasionally overwhelming sexual urges that afflict us all in our youth. These spells should not ever be considered love spells, as they are strictly lust spells. My favorite spell of this nature, of which I have heard nothing but good reports, is the following:

The Red Candle Lust Spell

Take a red candle, a red birthday candle will do fine, and light it with a sincere prayer that you find someone with whom to have sexual intercourse. Now after the candle burns out, or even while it is still burning, you should go out and look for the kind of person with whom you want to have sexual relations. Every time I have heard a complaint about this spell not working, it was because the person did not go out looking for the sexual contact that they had just said that they wanted, and for which they had just prayed.

You might not find just what you want in a sexual partner, but you will usually find someone to have sexual relations with if you go out looking for someone after performing this simple spell. As I have said, this is not a love and romance spell, it is strictly a spell to have sex with someone. Please bear that in mind if you decide to use it.

You should also bear in mind the old adage that a woman can always find someone to have sexual relations with, while a man can usually find someone with whom to have sexual relations. In either case, the person you find to have sexual relations with may not be your first choice, or your ideal mate, but by making use of this spell you will usually be able to find someone to solve the problem of your overwhelming sexual urges. You must be aware that the person you find for sexual release will probably be looking for the same kind of release that you are. They will probably not be interested in any kind of long-term relationship either.

Raising the Base Passions

An old Italian woman, who told me that as this spell was only useful for raising the base passions, she had no further use for it, gave this spell to me. I have found this spell to be useful for those who are neglectful of their mates, as well as for those who seem to have completely lost the feeling of joy and happiness in their life. Whether we wish to admit it to ourselves or not, most of us live our lives through our so-called base passions. When these passions grow weak in us, we may often go so far as to lose the will to live. In this case, this spell usually provides only temporary relief, but it often enables the person to change their viewpoint long enough to be able to seek the psychological assistance and counseling that they really require.

Take a half a teaspoon of ground sesame seed, and a tablespoon of fresh un-brewed ground coffee. Add a hair or other trace from the person whose passions are to be raised, even a strand of your own hair if that is what is desired. Mix the ingredients together well. Then pray over the mixture for the effect desired, and seal it in a closed container, like a small cardboard pillbox, or an envelope. This spell should be stored away as the effect, although often startling, is not usually very long lasting. Once you have achieved your goal for yourself or the other person, you should take the hair or other trace out of the spell, and wash it for a few moments in cold running water. You may then throw the coffee and sesame seed away, putting them into either the garbage or the toilet, as you prefer. It should be obvious to the neophyte magician, but materials used in one magical spell should not be reused in another.

Regaining a Lost Love

First, before you attempt this spell, think hard. Are you sure that you want your lost love back in your life? Remember, both of you have changed over the time you have been apart, no matter how long or how short a time it has been. Once you are sure that you want them back, the following spell will accomplish this for you, if there is any desire at all within them to return to you. On the other hand, if there is no desire for you within them at all, the spell will not work, and you will know that the romance between the two of you is permanently over. It is then time for you to let go of them, both mentally and emotionally, and just move on with the rest of your life.

Take an equal measure of ground Clove, Cinnamon, and Cardamom. A tablespoon of each is more than enough. Place these in a jar or pan, and pray over them for the return of your lost love, calling your lost love by name. Fill the jar or pan with rosewater, covering over the spices. Now add a piece of parchment or heavy writing paper that has the name of your lost love written clearly on it. In the corners of this paper, write the names of the four apostles, Matthew, Mark, Luke, and John. As you write the names of the apostles, pray to each of them to help return your lost love to you. Now place this mixture over a slow fire, and bring it to a boil. Allow the mixture to boil briefly. A half a minute is quite enough. Then take the container off the fire, and allow the mixture to cool to room temperature. Place the mixture in a jar, and hide it away. If you decide to repeat the spell, you should add the new mixture to the old, allowing the mixture to accumulate.

I have found that performing this spell on three consecutive new moons has a far better result than just doing it once and forgetting about it. Of course, as I have mentioned above, if your lost love has no desire at all to return to you, this spell or any other is quite unlikely to ever bring them back to you, or even have them contact you again. If this spell is going to work for you at all, your lost love will contact you in some way within six months time after you first perform it.

A Marriage Spell

A woman used this spell to ensnare a man who was briefly a client of mine. I had warned him that the woman he was seeing would use magic to get him to marry her, but he was quite sure that he was above all such non-physical influences. He had only come to see me to get a charm for his business, one like I had made for one of his business associates. As a clinical psychologist, he believed that his intellectually based rational scientific training gave him positive protection against any and all forms of magic, as well as against any other baleful influences that anyone might cast upon him. His business associate later told me that he was married to the woman within the year.

The spell the woman used was both quite common and very simple, and I have mentioned one variety of this spell, as a love spell, in my book '*A Century Of Spells*,' on page 105. The marriage spell given below is only a slight modification of the love spell given in my earlier book. This is an example of how spells may be slightly changed to suit different intentions.

The woman who wanted him to marry her took two sewing needles of the same size, ordinary needles that she had used in her sewing. She laid them together, with the point of one to the eye of the other. Then she tied the needles together with a white thread, a red thread, and a green thread. She then wrapped up the needles in a tissue paper in which she had sprinkled the powder of comfrey root herb. She put the wrapped package away in her underwear drawer, where my client found it after he had been married to the woman for about two years.

My client brought the packet to me, and as he told me that he was very unhappy in the marriage, I broke the spell by breaking the needles and dumping the entire packet of contents of the spell into a glass of holy water. The woman who had cast the spell on him left him before the end of the month. They were divorced shortly thereafter, something that was quite expensive for the man.

The colors of threads traditionally used for doing permanent marriage spells of all kinds, are white for fidelity and permanence, red for mutual passion and love, and green for prosperity and offspring. As an example of the milder form of this spell, when using this charm as a love spell, the two needles are wrapped with a comfrey leaf, or another green leaf that has been newly picked. The needles are then tied together with red yarn, and placed into a red charm bag.

Two needles tied with red yarn may be prepared as a general love spell, or more realistically, as a general sex attracting charm, for a person who desires to have such a thing. While this charm works quite well, those who are sexually promiscuous do not recommend it for use by those who are not. It is useful for drawing the kind of temporary sex partner usually known as a one-night stand.

Strawberry Marriage Spell

Fresh strawberries and cream have been said to be the food of the honeymooners. Strawberry oil, perfume, or incense, lightly applied in a room, gives a slight 'bridal chamber' atmosphere to the room. Naturally, this may be used either for inducing marriage or for expediting a seduction. I recommend it to for women to use in their homes when they wish to encourage a man to take their already close relationship to the next step of commitment, whether the man feels ready to do so or not. Strawberry perfume or incense is usually quite effective when it is used in this way. Of course, the woman should also be ready to take the next step toward intimacy in their relationship.

Another Love Spell

In most cases, the woman who is seeking a mate wishes to 'catch' her man in the same way that a fisherman catches a fish. The same language is frequently used to describe both events. The following spell takes advantage of this verbal symbolism, and directly aids the one wishing to make the 'catch' whether male or female, aiding them to 'land' their desired mate.

Write the name of the person that you wish to 'catch' on a piece of paper. The paper should be trimmed so it is no larger than the name, with only a slight edge around the written name. Now hook five small fishhooks into the person's name, concentrating on your catching them as you do so. Next, write your name on another piece of paper, and cut it to about the same size or a slight bit larger than the first piece of paper. Place the name with the fishhooks in the bottom of a small bottle, like a baby food jar. Add about a tablespoon of honey over the name that contains the fishhooks. Now place the piece of paper with your name written on it on top of the honey. Lastly, put a small amount of honey on top of your name. Now pray over the open jar that you be able to 'catch' the one you wish, 'landing them' and making them your mate. Mention both yourself and them by name in your sincere prayer. Then cap the jar and hide it away. This is another spell that has gathered a reputation for success with a great many people. It is quite popular, and even has developed a number of variations.

One of the more interesting virtues of this spell is that you can put an end to the spell by simply flushing the contents of the jar down the toilet, once you have decided that you no longer want to have the person you have cast this spell upon in your life. This makes it a particularly good love spell when used by those who are fickle lovers. A young lady told me she had flushed this spell into the toilet while talking to her lover on the telephone. She told me that his impassioned pleas to her turned to complete indifference as she spoke to him, immediately after she had flushed the spell away.

A Variation of the Above Spell

To make yourself attractive to a particular person, but not necessarily to become their lover, place the names of the two people in honey, as above, but without using fishhooks. Be sure that your name is placed on top of the other person's name. Baby food jars are perfect for this work, as are small cold cream or ointment jars, however, you should wash them thoroughly first.

Once the names are in the jar with honey, you may add a drop or two each of Jasmine, Cinnamon, Sweet Pea, and Rose Oils to the bottle. Any of these oils will assist the spell to work in a more romantic manner. Pray over the bottle that the person you desire be strongly attracted to you, and if you wish, ask that they become your lover. You do not ask for this if it is not what you want. You must use both of your names when you make your prayer. Once the prayer is finished, just close up the bottle and hide it away.

This spell is also useful in gaining the favorable attention of superiors at your work place, but if you are not interested in forming a sexual relationship with them, do not add any of the perfume oils. In this case, just use about a teaspoon of honey between the two names that you place in the bottle. On the other hand, you can prepare the spell with just honey, and add the oils later, if you decide that you now wish the person to become your lover.

Still Another Love Spell

Love spells are legion in number. There are so many of them that several books have been written that deal only with love spells. The following love spell is one that was recommended to me many years ago by a Hindu lady. She told me with a smile that it was her favorite love spell. She said that it had the advantage of being able to be undone, like the previous love spell that used honey and fishhooks. I suppose that being able to undo the love spell you have caught your lover with, once you tire of them, is a great advantage to those who prefer to have variety in their love life. Like the previous spell, this spell is one that may be done to get either a man or a woman as a lover for the person who is performing it.

Take a piece of writing paper and write the name of the person you desire upon it three times. Then turn the paper a quarter turn in a clockwise direction and write your name over theirs three times, making an equal limbed cross of the two names. Now take three or four whole coriander seeds, (from the grocery store) and holding them in your right hand, (If you are right handed, in your left hand if you are left handed) pray over the seeds that you have the person whose name you have written on the paper as your lover. You should mention both your name, and the name of the person who you wish to have as your lover in your prayer. Place the seeds on the paper, directly over the crossed names. Next, cover the names and the seeds with red powder. (Binney and Smith red powdered water paint, ground powdered red chalk, or Indian red Kum-kum powder, you have your choice of which kind of powder you wish to use, it makes no difference.) Roll up the paper, doing your best to keep the seeds and the powder inside. You will have to twist the ends of the paper to keep everything in place. Finally, tie the paper closed around the center, using a piece of iron wire.

You now have a small paper package that looks like one of those old-fashioned taffy candies. Place this package into a small bottle, and add some camphor, say a piece as large as your thumbnail, and about an eighth of an inch thick or so. It is not necessary to use a whole cube of camphor. Place the lid on the bottle, and close it up tight. Now hide the bottle away somewhere where it is unlikely to be discovered by your lover or by anyone else.

To undo this spell, take the paper package out of the bottle, undo the iron wire, and wash the names on the paper with cold running water. Throw everything connected with the spell into the garbage, wet paper, coriander seeds, red powder, iron wire, and even the bottle that held the spell. Remove the garbage from your home immediately.

A Bath for A Woman Seeking Love

This bath is designed to attract a lover to a woman, but it will work better for her if the universe provides the lover, rather than the bath being taken to catch a specific man whom the woman has in mind. Make a bath using five yellow roses, some river water, and a tablespoon of honey. The woman taking the bath should soak in the bath for ten minutes or more, praying in the bath that she find the kind of lover whom is seeking. The more clear and accurate an idea that the woman has of what she wants in a lover, the more likely she is to actually obtain what she is looking for.

I usually recommend that any person seeking a permanent relationship take the time to write out exactly what they are looking for in a lover before they begin doing any kind of magical work to bring one to them. Just as in all other fields of human endeavor, advance planning and setting a fixed goal always pays off for the one who does so. One of the big secrets in magic is that once you really know exactly what you want, you are already at least half way toward actually obtaining it for yourself.

An Attraction Bath

This is a general attraction bath, and may be taken by a woman for that purpose, as well as for either finding a new lover, or for encouraging your current lover to propose marriage to you.

Steep equal quantities of Hyssop herb and Sweet Balm in river or lake water for seven days. Put the herbs in a mason jar, add the water, and then put the jar in the refrigerator for a week or so. Add the herbs and water to a tub bath, and bathe for seven minutes. While in the tub you should pray for just what you want, either that someone be attracted to you, or that a specific person become your lover, or for a specific person (who you have been dating—

and you are in contact with) to propose marriage to you. In the tub immerse yourself seven times, and be sure to air dry when you leave the tub. Do not bathe again for twenty four hours. Put the spell out of your mind, so that you can let go of it and allow the spell to do its work.

A Magnet Oil Love Spell

If you have no one person in mind, but just wish to draw a lover or a mate to you, anointing a candle with magnet or lodestone oil will help in this effort. This is an oil available in Botanicas and some spiritual supply stores that has small pieces of magnetic iron in it. It must have these small bits of magnetic iron in the bottle to be real magnet oil. Red candles are used for love spells, but white or blue candles should be used for marriage spells. As love or lust usually comes before marriage rather than afterwards, red candles are usually used for this work.

Anoint the lower half of the candle from the middle to the bottom, and the upper half from the middle to the top. Then light the candle, and pray that you attract a lover or a mate to yourself. Which you pray for depends on what you really want in your life. You should have thought this over, and come to a firm decision before you began this spell.

As with all other general love spells of this kind, you must now go out and try to find yourself a lover. You must socialize; making a real effort to meet new people, and doing your very best to make new friends. No love spell will attract anyone to you when you are sitting at home alone in your room. General love spells always work far better than those that are aimed at catching a particular person. This is because the universe, while quite willing to provide anyone with a lover, is usually very unlikely to send you the particular person that you may have in mind, or the one that you desire to have as a lover. Unless you are a movie star, you are unlikely to have a movie star for a lover, much less for a marriage partner. Be realistic in what you ask for and you will be far more likely to get it.

Lodestone Attraction Spell

Lodestones have been used since antiquity for attracting material things to people. As a living breathing lover is certainly a material thing, you can use a lodestone to attract a lover. Take a lodestone and wrap it with a piece of paper on which you have written out your desires for a lover, using as few words as possible. When you are looking for a lover, the paper should contain all of your requirements for the lover whom you desire to attract to yourself. Now carry the lodestone with you, knowing that it will do its best to attract what you wish to you. If you wish to further empower the lodestone spell, you should place one drop of lodestone oil on it for each year if your life before you wrap it up in the paper.

This spell may also be used for attracting other material things to you as well. One young lady wrapped the lodestone in a photograph of an automobile that she wanted to own. She was able to purchase the car at a very reasonable price about two months later.

Love Spells Using Photographs

Love spells using sketches or drawings of the people who were the desired beloved seem to have an ancient history. As photography is a very recent technique in magical work, these spells are actually a modern continuation of older spells using sketches and drawings. Of course, the photographs provide a far more accurate representation of both the lover and the beloved than crude sketches or drawings ever could. The following spells have all been used successfully, and I recommend them to you, if you both know whom you wish to attract, and have a photograph available of your beloved.

Making Your Lover 'Sweet on You'

Cement two photographs, one of the lover and one of the beloved face to face, using a few drops of honey as the glue. With a table knife pressed on the back of the photographs, make sure that honey covers both of the people, cementing the photographs together. Once the photographs are cemented together, roll them up into a tube, and wrap a red thread around the tube at least nine times. Now tie the tube in place, so it will not straighten out again. Place this tube away, realizing that in time it will make the other person become as sweet on you as you already are on them.

When a Love Spell Works

When you do a love spell of any kind on another person, you must now be open to them. Should they begin a conversation with you, you must respond to it actively, and should they ask you for a date, even casually offering to just have coffee or lunch with you, you should immediately agree. You have taken the initiative by performing the spell. Now you must be compliant to them, making yourself available to them for any social contact that they may attempt to initiate with you.

Women work most magical spells for love, then they often void the effort of the spell by being overly nervous or reluctant about accepting social invitations when the man they are seeking to ensnare, or any other man, asks them out. If a woman wants the man for a lover, she certainly should be able to accept an invitation from him for a date or some other social contact. He is not going to become close to her unless she allows their social contact to occur.

The same difficulty is found among men who are shy, or those who are fearful of women. Worshiping a woman from afar, these men could often develop a friendship, if not a romance with the woman if they would just speak to them. I am always amazed that these men do not just open a casual conversation with the woman in whom they are interested. The worst thing that the woman can do is ignore them, but even in that case they are really no worse off than they were before.

About thirty years ago, I had a client who was more than just stunningly beautiful. An actress, she was often seen in the company of male actors who had an underground reputation of being sexually uninterested in women. She once told me that she could not find a decent heterosexual man who would even approach her for a date. It seems that all of the men that she was interested in were afraid of her great beauty. Apparently, these men did not have the self-confidence to even ask her out socially.

In time, she married a man who was several years older than her, and more of a dynamic warrior like character than the actor he actually worked at being. I met him once, and he admitted to me that he had never felt fear in his life. If that is what it takes to approach a truly beautiful woman today, I fear that most men, and most of these stunningly beautiful women, are in serious trouble.

If you decide to do a love spell to attract someone you are drawn to, please be open to the spell you have performed actually bearing fruit. Do not allow your fear of your beloved to block you from socializing with them, especially should they ask you to join them for any social event, from coffee to an evening on the town. This is particularly true for women, but it is also true for men who use love spells in an attempt to attract their chosen beloved to them.

Keeping Your Beloved Thinking About You

This spell may be done whether you wish to keep them with you, or when you just wish to plague the person with thoughts of you. In the latter case, it may be considered to be a bit of malefic magic, but I suppose that in these cases it is still a worthwhile thing for a jilted or abandoned lover to do. I first used this spell in the case of a man who had recently fired his secretary, who was one of my students. He had made inappropriate sexual advances to her, and had fired her when she refused to yield to him. She wished to obtain a kind of mild vengeance on him, keeping him thinking about her, so together we worked this spell on him.

She had two photographs of him that had been taken at a company Christmas party. She also had six enticing nude photographs of herself that a former boy friend had taken of her some years previously. From the nude photographs of her, using scotch tape, we made a box with her photographs facing inside, as well as forming the floor and ceiling of the small box of photographs. The photographs of her former boss were glued back to back, and suspended inside the box with a thread, so that no matter which way his photograph turned inside the box, it would always be facing a nude photograph of her. We then prayed over the assembly that thoughts of her would haunt him.

She took this arrangement home and hid it away it in a hatbox in her closet. Within a week, her former boss began calling her, asking her to return to work. She had already obtained a better position, but his calls persisted. To end these calls, which eventually became quite annoying to her, she finally had to disassemble the spell. Obviously, this spell may be done to keep someone you are interested in thinking about you in either romantic or quite ordinary terms, depending on the kind of photographs that you use, and the prayer that is made over the assembled object.

A Binding Spell

The purpose of this spell is to gain control over another person. This kind of control is easily obtained over only a very few people, who happen to be susceptible to both the spell and to the spell caster. Thus, this spell must be repeated time and time again, and you must see some real results of your work in your relationship with the other person, before you may assume that it has even begun to achieve its intended purpose. With that caveat in mind, this spell has proven itself quite useful for many people.

Naturally, a well-trained magician can use this spell more successfully than other people can, but I have seen untrained people be surprisingly successful with this spell, because they worked at using it religiously. In one case, a woman used it for six months and managed to get her husband, who had more than a roaming eye, to cease directing most of his attentions to other women. Because of the successes, I have seen with this spell, even when used by people without any magical training at all, I include it here for your use, should you think it appropriate to your circumstances. Please remember that you must be persistent and dedicated in using it to have real success with it.

Obtain a photograph of the person who is to be bound to the one doing the spell. The photograph may not be in a picture frame. The person doing the spell must be able to hold the photograph in their hand, and concentrate all of their attention on it while doing the spell.

Now to perform this spell, the person performing it looks at the photograph and speaks the following words over and over again, seeing these words enter into the mind of the person they are seeking to influence.

"Thou shall be obedient to me so long as this life shall empower thee. Thy mind shall hear my every command, and thou shall follow them, both subtle and grand.

Thy will shall completely bend to mine, and thou shall serve me at my request and time."

If you wish to do so, you can modernize this spell a bit. It originally came from a 16th century hand written spell book, where it was to be done with a sketch of the person. The important thing is that the spell be done every day for at least six months, probably even longer. It is the constant repetition of this spell that gradually bears fruit. You also must wait until the person you are working on indicates a desire to follow your leadership in some way before assuming that the spell you have cast is actually working for you. I might add that the best magicians I know will take at least a month to obtain any results at all with this spell, even focusing their mind and will into performing it every night. Do not be discouraged if it takes you longer than six months to accomplish anything visible to you while you are using it. Your perseverance will pay dividends for you, but the ultimately successful results will come only over a rather long period.

To Break The Affections

This spell may only be used to break off your affectionate relationship with someone else. It will not break up another couple, so you cannot use it to get to someone who is married, or someone who is involved with someone else. This is an important point, because breaking up other people's relationships seems to be one of the things that many people like to do magically. This spell just will not do that for you.

On the other hand, if you are really tired of going to the movies every Saturday night with dear old so and so, and you have decided that you just won't make it as a couple, or that you don't want to go any further with them, this is a very good way to cause the relationship to painlessly disintegrate.

Take about a teaspoon full of basil herb and a teaspoon full of rue herb. Mix them together well and pray over them that your relationship with dear old so and so come to an end, painlessly and without any difficulty on either side. You must mention both your name and the name of the other party in the prayer. You may add why you want the relationship to come apart if you wish, although this is not always necessary. Once you have finished your prayer, you should burn the mixed herbs on charcoal in your living quarters. Open a window so that the fumes from the burning herbs go out into the universe. Usually the relationship will fall apart within a week of your doing this spell.

Warning: Don't try and hold on to the relationship! Once you do this spell. You have committed yourself to letting your relationship with the other person go and be put behind you. Once you perform the spell you must completely let go of the relationship, both mentally and emotionally. Otherwise, you will be in for a serious heartache and more emotional stress.

To Cause Strife Between People

This spell causes strife and arguments between two people. It is useful when you want your girlfriend and her boyfriend, whom you disapprove of, to fight. It will not usually break them up, but it will cause tension, strife, and argument, in their relationship, or in any other relationship, romantic or not.

Take the seeds of two dried hot peppers and write the names of the two people on two separate pieces of paper. Twist the seeds of one hot pepper in one paper, and the seeds of the other hot pepper in the other paper. Place both papers on the stove in a saucepan or frying pan, and heat them up. Do not allow the papers to burn, just heat them for a brief time until they are hot to the touch. Then let them cool and put the cool papers away. You can re-heat these papers whenever you wish to increase the tension and strife between the two people.

Lightening The Emotions Of Love

With all of these love spells it is no wonder that you frequently feel the heavy emotions engendered by love to be wearing on you. To lighten yourself from all the trauma of love, especially the trauma of will he or won't he, you should take a bath in basil tea. Make up a basil tea by adding a teaspoon of basil herb to a cup of boiling water. Turn off the heat, and allow the tea to reach room temperature. Once the water reaches room temperature, you can add it to a tub of lukewarm water and soak in the tub for six minutes while immersing yourself six times and praying for relief from the pangs of love.

If you wish, you can make up a basil alcohol in much the same manner. This involves putting about two teaspoons of cooking basil into a bottle of rubbing alcohol, preferably ethyl rubbing alcohol, but the more common isopropyl rubbing alcohol will work just as well. Shake the bottle to mix the herb and alcohol thoroughly. Now put it aside for a week or so, shaking it well every day. Strain the herb out of the tincture after a week. To use this basil alcohol, put some of the alcohol on a cotton ball and wipe it on the back of your neck.

To use the mixture in a bath, add twice the volume of river water to the basil mixture, and add this to a tub bath. Soak in the bathtub for eight to ten minutes, immersing yourself five times or more while praying to be relieved of the emotional upsets and pressures of love.

If you are fickle in your affections, or know that you are deeply emotional, you might wish to make the basil sprinkle up in advance, just to be prepared for the inevitable emotional trauma that is sure to follow your falling in love again.

CHAPTER FOUR

Spells Dealing With Obnoxious Or Hateful People

About Difficult People

It would be nice if we could all get along with each other all of the time. Unfortunately, both people and nations have disagreements, quarrels, and even open battles from time to time. We are only really expected to be polite and civil to each other, as the ideal of our really loving each other as we love ourselves is an impractical un-realty for the great bulk of humanity. Perhaps at some golden time in the future things will be better, but for now we have to live with what we find in other people, as well as having to live with what we may have discovered hiding deep within ourselves.

It would be really wonderful if we could all interrelate with each other without becoming emotionally involved. Unfortunately, some people seem to delight in dragging others into their personal emotional quagmire. We should always do our best to avoid falling into the emotional quagmire of others, as well as consciously avoid dragging other people into our own emotional quagmire. If we can do so, we will be free of at least half of the energy that we usually waste on these ultimately petty emotional distractions.

What we usually find from time to time, both in the work place and in our social activities, are the occasional few people who are envious or jealous of others. These people are generally disagreeable, and even hateful toward those they envy. Occasionally we may find one of these negative people focusing their internal negativity directly toward us.

We do not have to accept the envy, jealousy, or even the directed negativity of these people. In fact, we can even work against their negativity in ways that they cannot ever know about. This chapter is about preventing these negative reactions in others, as well as about taking direct action against any negativity we may feel coming to us from others, when it does occur.

Preventing Jealousy And Oppression

The easiest way to prevent emotions of jealousy and oppression being directed against you is to take two or three heaping tablespoons of talcum powder and add a level quarter teaspoon of powdered cinnamon to it. Mix these two ingredients thoroughly. Place the mixed powder in a small bottle, like a baby food bottle or the like. Shaking the bottle well will mix them together just fine. Every morning, before you go to work, place a dab of this well mixed powder on your sternum, or breastbone.

You do not need to use a lot of this powder, just about as much as would make a kitchen match head or so will be all you need for the day. Apply the powder after you bathe, and then just dress normally. I have found this to be a very successful way to banish many of the petty jealousies and quarrels of daily life, and especially those frictions, tensions, and jealousies that often surround the work place.

Keeping Off Negative Influences

One of the easiest ways to avoid having to live in the kind of negativity that you find on the streets and at the work place is to keep yourself physically clean. Taking a shower after work and changing from your working clothes will remove many of the generally negative influences or 'vibrations' that people pick up from time to time in their daily activities. If you make it a practice to do this as soon as you come home, and before you try and deal with the stresses of the day, the problems of your spouse, or the concerns of your children, you will find that you will be able to approach these domestic matters in a considerably more calm and controlled manner.

If you make it a family rule that everyone must shower and change into clean clothes after returning home from any outside activities, you will find that many of the annoying but petty things that people think have happened to them during the day, will have dissipated. They have gone down the drain with the shower.

While you are in the shower, running some cool water on the back of the neck has proven to be quite effective in clearing away many of the obstacles and difficulties which people think they have had in the workplace that day. That and some cool water running on the sternum, between the breasts, will alleviate many of the difficulties of a hard day at work, at school, or even out shopping at the mall. This is actually a very good program for any family to follow. It assures you that you and the members of your family will not be carrying around the petty but disturbing negative influences from workplace, school, or wherever else you may have been during the day. Removing these minor disturbing influences will always make your home life easier, and more tranquil.

Obnoxious People

Almost every work place has some obnoxious people in it. Sometimes it is the supervisor; most often it is another employee. It really does not matter who the obnoxious person is, the method given below will help you get them away from you, or at least take away from them any power over you that you may have accidentally granted them. This system acts to moderate the hateful attitude that some people seem to have toward everyone around them as well.

Please notice that there are two steps to this process, both of which should be used in extreme or long lasting cases. In simple cases, the first remedy will usually be found to work after using it for two or three weeks. When the first remedy does not work, you may go on to the second remedy, for an even stronger effect.

Remedy #1

Take a piece of blank scrap paper. Write the name of the hateful person on the paper, and place it in your shoe. If you are right handed, place the paper in your right shoe. If you are left handed, place the paper in your left shoe. Should you find yourself talking with the person during the day, either in person or on the telephone, quietly and gently tap your foot on the ground as you speak to them.

After you have done this for two or three weeks, and if you sense that there has been no let up at all in their belligerent attitude, begin placing the paper with their name on it in your other shoe. Give this modification of the spell another two or three weeks. If there is still no letup on their part, you may go on to doing the second remedy, but you still should continue to keep putting the obnoxious person's name in your left shoe (if you are right handed).

Remedy #2

Once you decide to go further, you must now keep a soft lead pencil on your person at all times. When you have to go to the toilet, write the obnoxious person's name on a single square of toilet paper, and then place the square of toilet paper in the bowl, and go to the toilet on it. Be sure to flush the evidence away. This has the effect of making the person gradually become increasingly repulsive to other people. This simple spell has been found to be quite an effective solution to problems of this kind over the course of many years. The two of these spells, when done together, have usually resulted in the person being isolated by others at work, and put in the position of not being believed when they make accusations or slurs against other people.

Clarifying Situations, At Work Or At Home

Obtain some dried hard corn, the kind known as Indian corn. This is often available on husks in the fall, usually around Halloween, when this kind of corn is frequently used for decoration. The corn may be either plain or the multicolored variety, it does not matter which. Crush the grains of corn in a mortar, or with a hammer. Once you have a handful of the crushed corn, toast it lightly in the oven. You want to toast the corn just a bit, do not bake the corn until it is really dark, or black.

Now get at least a dozen white eggshells, which have had the membrane next to the shell removed. Grind the eggshells into a fine powder, either in the mortar or by using a rolling pin on a cookie sheet. Mix the powdered eggshells with the ground corn, and place the resulting course powder into a bottle. Shake the bottle vigorously, blending the ingredients together well.

When you have a problem with another person, whether at work or at home, sprinkle some of this powder around the area you are occupying. This could be your desk, your workstation, or your easy chair. Ideally, you will be able to spread the powder around a place that is generally identified as yours. In your own home, you should place some of this powder; say a quarter teaspoon full or less, in the corners of the rooms of your house as well. You may have to repeat the scattering of this powder several times, so you should be prepared to do so.

In a short time, usually within a few days to a week, the problem will become more clear, and then you will be able to work your way out of it. Sometimes doing this spell will cause the apparent problem to completely clear up, seemingly all by itself.

Putting Problems Behind You

When you discover that you have a problem or a difficulty in your life, whether another person causes it or not, there is an effective way to literally put this problem behind you. In a way it is something like 'kissing the problem up to God,' but this is actually a more physical solution to the problem.

First, write out the problem. Take your time, and get the problem that is facing you written out exactly as you understand it. This process should take you some serious thought and time, but it must not be rushed, as it is the true key to permanently eliminating the difficulty. Write the problem out carefully, and be sure that you have written it out exactly as you understand it.

This process is called the objectification of the problem or the difficulty that you are facing. Once you know exactly what the problem or difficulty really is, and have objectified it to the best of your ability using as few words as possible, a solution to the problem might just suddenly present itself to you.

If you still see no solution to the difficulty, place the sheet of paper with the problem written out in it into a can full of ground coffee. Then hide the can away in your closet, or somewhere else out of sight. Give it at least a few weeks or a month. You will discover that the solution to the problem will gradually appear. Once the solution appears to you, the end of the problem or difficulty you have objectified is in sight at last.

Getting The Final Word

Sometimes we just have to have the final word with someone. This often happens when a friendship or a romantic relationship suddenly and unexpectedly breaks up. In not a few cases, the person whom we wish to have the final word with has already left our life, and there is either no way that we can contact them, or we do not wish to contact them in person again. So long as we believe that the person is alive, there is a way that we can get 'the final word' to them out of our system.

Begin by writing a letter to the person, putting into it everything that you have to say to them. If you have strong emotions about them, express these emotions both as you write the letter, and in the letter. In so far as is possible, get everything you wish to say to them, or tell them, completely out of your system. Once you have finished writing the letter, fold it up and place it into an envelope.

Now put about a tablespoon of ground coffee into the envelope, both into and on the letter. Seal the envelope and put it into a corner of the main room in your living quarters. Leave the letter there for a week or two, and then throw it into the garbage. The letter, for all practical purposes, has been delivered to the person that you wrote it to. This occurs through a process known as transference, where the emotional force of one person is transferred to another.

Unloading, Or Speaking Your Mind To Someone

It is not unusual to become highly irritated at someone to whom you dare not tell your real feelings. One of my students was in an Army Reserve unit, and although he was an officer, his commander treated him and several of the other young officers as if they were mentally retarded. After two weeks of this treatment during his annual drill, he came back hopping mad at the commander, and of course, unable to say anything at all to his face. I suggested the following technique to him. He performed it satisfactorily, and was quite pleased with the results.

Take a glass of water and two candles, and set the glass between the two candles. Now write the name of the person you wish to address, and place it under the glass of water. If it is at all possible, place their picture behind the glass. Light the candles, and then speak your mind to the glass of water, venting all of the anger you feel toward the person, and mentioning anything that comes to your mind about them. As all of your anger pours out, you may find that things come up that you had not even connected to the person you are addressing. Just let everything all come out, making notes if you wish of what it is that you are bringing up, and dealing with. Once you have got all out of this emotion out of yourself, you will feel much better.

To your own benefit you may even have generated a pad of notes for your private self-examination work. The most important thing is that your negative emotions are no longer bottled up inside you. Just allow the candles to burn out and then pour the water into the toilet, rinsing the glass out three times, as you would with your night water.

If you wish, you can pour the water from the glass where the person you spoke to will pass by. Sometimes the residual emotion that you have placed into the water will consciously affect them.

Keeping People Off Of Your Back

Some people seem to be just naturally obnoxious, or even vile. In some cases, these are people who have been given some little authority, and who seem to have gone wild with the supposed power of their position. These people may become like the proverbial monkey on your back, constantly deliberately doing things that seem to be designed just to aggravate and annoy you.

Such was the case with the new sanitation inspector in my neighborhood. He constantly harassed myself and the other tenants of my building about our garbage. We were not responsible for putting it out, that task was the building superintendents. Despite this, the sanitation inspector would write all of us tickets, each of them requiring us to pay a fine of $25.00. He wrote these tickets if the garbage was put out even a few minutes before six in the morning each day. After receiving two of these tickets or summons, which I could ill afford, I decided to do something about the man. His name was on the ticket he had given me, so I copied it down on a piece of scrap paper, actually a small piece of paper I had torn from a paper garbage bag.

I put that paper along with a bit of camphor and some salt into a small plastic paint container that had once held a few ounces of water paint. I added about a tablespoon full or so of water, and then put it into the freezer compartment of my refrigerator. I left the container sitting there for several days. The building superintendent met me on the morning of the fourth or fifth day after I had done this spell, and told me that the overly enthusiastic sanitation inspector had been transferred to another location. On returning home that day, I took the container out of the freezer and threw it into the garbage. I and the other tenants of my building never received any more of those annoying and costly sanitation tickets.

A Lesser Spell For People Who Are Annoying

Instead of putting the container in the freezer, or if you do not have a small plastic container that will take the expansion of the water as it freezes, you can put the name along with some camphor and a pinch of salt into a small dark glass bottle. Then add some water, and hide the bottle away in a dark place for some time. Should you do this, it is best if you replace the camphor and water every three or four days, or at least every week. You can flush the old material down the toilet, and use the same bottle with some new camphor, salt, and a new piece of paper with the person's name written on it. This spell works equally well against these troubling and obnoxious people. This version of the spell does require considerably more personal attention directed to maintaining the spell.

Souring A Person's Life

When someone does something nasty to you, you may wish to strike back with an equally nasty retribution. If you are certain this is what you wish to do, the following spell will produce the results that you want.

Take a lemon and slice a deep slit in it, half way through it, cutting the lemon lengthwise. Write the name of the person whose life you wish to sour on a piece of paper, and insert the paper in the lemon. Now place the lemon in the refrigerator, and leave it for several weeks, until the lemon begins to turn quite hard. When the lemon begins to turn hard, take it out, wash the name off with cold water, and then throw both the lemon and the name into your garbage container.

If you really do not want to sour the person's life, but

just want the person to leave you alone, use a cucumber instead of a lemon. In most cases, the cucumber will do the trick, and only if the person persists in annoying you will you need to go on to using a lemon.

Keeping People Away From You

This spell is useful to keep away people who wish to impose themselves on you, and often seem to desire nothing more than to make you their best friend, frequently against your will. The powder made from crushed dried poplar leaves may be held in your hand and prayed over to hide yourself from those who would find you. If you live anywhere near a poplar tree, it is usually worthwhile to get some of these leaves, dry them, and just have the powder on hand, in the event that you ever need to use this spell. It works well against specific people who wish to find you, but it is not nearly as effective against bill collectors and those others who have a legal right to know your whereabouts.

If you know the name of the person or persons you wish to keep away from you, you should use their names in the prayer. Once you have prayed over the powder, blow some of the powder out of each of the doors and windows of your home or apartment. Blowing a pinch of the powder will do as much good as using any larger quantity.

A typical prayer useful for this purpose is:

> _Name_ I cover your path to me.
> You cannot find me,
> Your thoughts cannot find me,
> I am now hidden from you.

To Make Someone Talk Indiscreetly

Take three parrot feathers—(try a pet shop for these). Write the name of the person you wish to talk indiscreetly on a small piece of paper. Get a tie to them, a hair, a photograph, or something similar. Wrap the paper around the tie to the person and the parrot feathers. Pray over this assemblage as to what you wish the person to say.

"I ask that _name_ talk to me (Or to someone else) fully and freely about _____ holding nothing at all back from me (or them) concerning this matter."

This is a good way to get at the truth about something when you believe that someone may be concealing the whole truth about something from you.

To Keep Someone From Talking

On the other hand, there are times when you don't want someone to talk, particularly if you believe that they may be indiscrete about saying something that you prefer to keep secret. This spoken spell works well for this purpose. You may speak it to the person, to their photograph, or to a trace of them. This spell has even been effectively used by speaking it in the direction where the person it was used against happened to be located at the time.

> Sealed thou art and sealed shall be;
> From now until I set thee free.
> Discretion sits upon thy lip,
> And will not let the wrong words slip.

Dealing With Crossed Conditions Or Curses

A crossed condition, malochia, or a curse is something that can make the life of the person who has it quite miserable. In the event that you feel that your luck has suddenly soured, or that your life has suddenly turned for the worse, you should treat it as if you have been the recipient of a minor curse. Sometimes a pain in your back c neck, or a metallic taste in your mouth tells you that you may have been the recipient of Malochia, the 'evil eye.'

There are a large number of 'do it yourself' remedies for Malochia that will generally eliminate, or at the very least, weaken the Malochia. This will allow you to seek any further help that may be required to remove it from you. The following instructions are taken directly from my book '*Spiritual Cleansing,*' on pages 16 & 17. I refer you to that book for more complete information, but there is sufficient information given here to allow you to take the bath mentioned herein successfully.

The first step in ridding yourself of any non-physical affliction is to take a beer bath. This is accomplished by pouring three bottles of beer into half a tub of lukewarm water. Add a teaspoon full of table salt, and stir the water clockwise until the beer and water are well mixed.

Then, enter the tub nude and immerse yourself completely several times. Sit in the tub and pour the water over yourself while you pray that all negativity you have on you, from whatever source it may originate, be permanently removed from you. Immerse and rinse yourself several more times, until you have been in the water six or seven minutes. You can use either a saucepan or a drinking glass to pour the water over your body as you sit in the tub.

Leave the tub and towel dry your hair, put on a bathrobe if you wish, but allow the bath water to dry on your body. You should go to your bedroom immediately and pray sincerely for help in remaining free of negativity. The best prayer you can make for this purpose is the Twenty Third Psalm. The Lord's Prayer, at Matthew 6:9-13, may be used by those who are believing Christians.

There is more information on breaking minor curses and keeping yourself spiritually clean in my books, '*Spiritual Cleansing,*' and '*Century of Spells.*' However, this procedure will weaken and remove from the victim almost all negative spells, and it will even take away serious attacks of malochia almost immediately.

Canceling Magical Spells

Most people who deliberately do negative magic are not trained magicians. As a result, their work, while it may be annoying and even hurtful, is not as completely destructive as they might wish it to be. When a trained magician performs any serious negative magic on someone, his or her victim will not realize that anything at all is wrong. Instead, they will just begin complying with the wishes of the magician; whatever they may happen to be. There is a vast difference in this and the attempts of an untrained and inexperienced person to lay curses, or to harm someone magically. I will also add that trained magicians usually are not at all interested in doing serious negative magic on people, especially those who have not attempted to harm them in some way first. Serious negative work, like serious magical work of any kind, requires a great deal of effort on the part of the magician. The trained magician will usually use one or more simple spells; such as I have given in this chapter, before going any further in working against someone.

Voiding Candle Magic

Many people use candle magic in their attempts to control others. It is actually the most common form of magical spell casting, as it is easy, simple, and it usually attains its goal. Sometimes these spells are just sent out into the universe. Other times, they are spells that are directed against a specific person. In all cases, there is a simple and effective way to negate this work. Wearing a small nail in your hair will reverse the effects of almost all candle magic. The kind of nail known as a four penny finishing nail can usually be easily concealed in a woman's hair. If you find this impossible to do during the workweek, you can wear the nail in your hair evenings and on weekends. As most candle magic seems to be done during the evenings and weekends, this is usually a satisfactory solution to the problem. If you wish to wear a nail in your hair at work, you can glue or tie the nail to a hairpin. One of my students received several compliments on her unusual hair ornament.

Some people cannot wear any metal in their hair, and if you are one of those people, you will not be able to use this simple spell. However, there is an even stronger spell for reversing this kind of magical work given below.

Reversing Negative Spells

This reversal spell is particularly good for reversing candle magic spells, but it will reverse many other negative spells as well. The least effect that the following spell will have is a considerable weakening of any negative work that has been done against the person who performs this spell. It is a very effective spell reversal, and one that I have used successfully for both others and for myself many times.

Arrange three candles in an equilateral or equal sided, triangle. This arrangement is known as burning candles in trinity. The base of the triangle should be nearest the person doing this spell reversal. The candles are lit in a counter clockwise direction; the left candle at the base of the triangle being lit first, then the right candle of the base, and lastly the point candle. If the person performing this spell is a believing Christian, they may light the candles in the name of 'God the Father, God the Son, and God the Holy Spirit.' Now break a fourth candle in half, and place it in the center of the triangle, with its wick to the left of the person who is performing this spell. The following prayer is to be made as the wick end of the fourth (broken) candle is placed into a candleholder and lit.

"May the force that is being used against me be broken and vanish into the night, just as I have broken this candle so that its smoke vanishes into the night."

Amen

In almost all cases the fourth (broken) candle will burn out first, and its smoke will vanish while the other three candles are still burning. If this does not occur, the spell should be repeated.

Getting People To Leave You Alone, When In Public

If you are being annoyed by anyone in a public place where alcoholic beverages are served, simply file a bit of your fingernail into their drink. Several women have assured me that this spell will cause the annoying person to leave you quickly. I must say that I have never done this, but this spell was mentioned to me by at least four different women, and they all recommend it. I pass it on to you for what it's worth, with the hope that you use it successfully.

Protecting Yourself From Negative People

One of my students gave me this spell, and I have used it for others on several occasions. It always seems to successfully protect the one using it from those who might try and impress their will on them. Take a photograph of the person you are seeking protection from, and a new spool of black sewing thread. Go for a walk, wrapping the black thread around the photograph of the person until you have wound the entire spool of black thread around the photograph. Now return home and place the photograph somewhere among your other finished spells, and forget about it. The person can no longer reach you with their thoughts or magic. This spell will work quite effectively on almost all people. The few it will not block completely will find their efforts considerably weakened if this spell is done. In one case, the person whose efforts had been seriously weakened by this spell even complained about it to the one who had done the spell!

Cleaning Yourself Of Strong Negative Influences From Others

Did you ever come home from work feeling as if you had just waded through a sewer? You feel dirty, but you know that it's not physical dirt that is annoying you. Usually a cool shower will assist you in ridding yourself of these negative feelings, but not always. When the feeling persists, even after a shower or a cleansing bath, its time to take the cleansing process a step further. A salt rub or salt glow will do this for you, as it will remove almost all of the generally negative influences from others that you may have picked up during the day. Simply rubbing your body with ordinary table salt, paying particular attention to rubbing salt on the back of your neck and on your sternum, the center of your chest, will often provide relief from this feeling of dinginess' or sludge surrounding you.

A cup of salt, rubbed all over your body, a tablespoon full at a time, will remove these feelings of 'crawling skin' and the non-physical ding or dirt that are caused by other peoples strong negativity and their projected self loathing.

If you wish to make up a more powerful mixture, especially if you have someone who can massage you with it, you can make up a mixture of equal quantities of Epsom Salt and Kosher salt. Kosher salt is just common salt but it has larger grains that provide more physical abrasion to the skin. Should this mixture be overly rough on your skin, you may add a slightly lesser amount of Baking Soda to the mixture. This will usually make it easier for sensitive skin to deal with.

I have had this salt rub recommended to me as a good preventative for colds and flue. I must admit that I prefer it for removing the dingy 'skin crawling' feeling I sometimes find that I have acquired when working with certain people. I have no idea if the salt rub will either treat or heal minor colds or flu. In any event, the salt rub is a good treatment to keep in mind as a way to cleanse yourself of external negativity brought by associating with these negative and self-loathing people who seem to wallow in that feeling.

CHAPTER FIVE

Spells Dealing With The Home Or Living Situation

The New Home Or Apartment

Moving into a new home or apartment usually carries with it a change in circumstances in the lives of the people who are making the move. Because any change in the circumstances needs to be made as comfortable and as beneficial as possible for the people involved, great care should be taken to make sure that the change of residence will actually be beneficial to them. Several things may be done to accomplish this. First is the thorough cleansing of the new quarters, to remove any physical and nonphysical traces of the former occupants. Then a beneficial atmosphere or a feeling compatible with the new occupants should be added to the living quarters.

Cleaning new homes or apartments always begins with a thorough physical cleaning of the new living space for you or your family. Adding a cup of household ammonia to a three gallon bucket of wash water will materially assist in removing grease, as well as in removing most of the heavy thought forms and other emotional residue found in most previously occupied living quarters. In addition to cleaning the floors, the walls of the new residence should be washed clean. While we usually think of washing the floors, many of us seem quite willing to cover dirty walls with a coat of paint. Thoroughly cleaning the walls will be as beneficial in cleaning the new living quarters as scrubbing the floors of their accumulated dirt and mental or emotional residue. If this residue is not removed, you will be forced to live with it so long as you occupy the quarters. It is always better to get rid of the residue before you move in.

 As with anything else, there is a best way or a best practice to wash floors and walls. Hospitals and some commercial buildings often use what is called a three-bucket system for washing these surfaces. In this system a wash bucket containing the cleaning solution is used, and is followed by two rinse buckets. The mop or washing sponge is rinsed twice, once in each rinse bucket. As the rinse water in the first rinse bucket becomes dirty, it is replaced. The second rinse bucket becomes the first rinse bucket, and the now clean water in the former first rinse bucket becomes the second rinse bucket.

 Because of using this three-bucket system, considerably more dirt is actually removed from the surface being cleaned than if a conventional one or two-bucket mopping operation were being done. I highly recommend this three-bucket system to you for at least the first washing of the walls and floors in any new residence you may desire to occupy. It will remove most of the dirt with one thorough mopping or scrubbing, instead of taking three or four separate moppings or scrubbings to do the task.

 Ammonia vaporizes thought forms, causing them to dissipate and disappear into the universe. I always advise adding ammonia to the wash water when you wet or damp mop any floor or wall. The only exception is for those people who absolutely cannot stand to work with ammonia at all. In that case, I think that it is worthwhile to hire someone to clean the apartment with ammonia for you. I would suggest that this is especially worthwhile the first time the living quarters are mopped or scrubbed clean.

Damp mopping on both furniture and rugs may be accomplished by using a dilute solution containing a cup of ammonia in about three gallons of wash water. Rapidly passing a damp sponge that has been wrung out in this ammonia wash water, with no soap or other additive in the water, will keep the rug or upholstery from being stained with non-physical stains.

Once the new residence has been thoroughly physically cleaned, a banishing incense such as dragon's blood can be burned to eliminate any of the negative vibrations that may still remain in the residence. When this incense is burned, all of the doors and windows of the residence should be opened. The doors may be opened only briefly, but the windows should be opened for the entire time that the dragon's blood incense is being burned. This is traditionally done to allow the negativity that the dragon's blood incense removes to leave the place. I also recommend doing this because of the odor of dragon's blood incense, which it seems, is obnoxious to many people.

When the washing and cleaning by incensing has been accomplished, the residence should be returned to a neutral state. At that point a purifying and blessing feeling should be put into the home. This is best accomplished by burning incense consisting of:

One part of Camphor, Two parts of crushed Myrtle leaves, and Three parts of Frankincense

This incense should be burned on charcoal. It places a more domestic and an only a slightly spiritual vibration into any newly occupied residence. The presence of this newer and higher vibration will often cause many of the remaining lesser negative vibrations remaining in the place to leave.

Burning this incense leaves a very warm and pleasant feeling in the home where it is burned, giving the home a nice domestic vibration. This same incense may be used any time you give your home a thorough physical and spiritual cleansing.

Unless you intend to dedicate your new residence to living a life of prayer and devotion, I do not recommend trying to make it overly 'spiritual.' While this may initially sound like it could be a good thing, in practice, it is highly unlikely that you will wish to live like an ascetic in your new quarters. Even those who are real ascetics usually desire to have feelings of happiness and joy surrounds them. You will also want to be able to continue your ordinary domestic and workday life, so a more domestic and only slightly spiritual incense is a much better choice to use than trying to turn your new home into a place of serious religious or spiritual dedication.

Indigo Blue Floor Wash

This floor wash is useful for purifying and strengthening any newly occupied quarters. It will seal a home or apartment against the accumulation of serious negativity, by strengthening its non-physical fabric. A single mopping of the floor of the new residence should provide the necessary strengthening of the residence for at least a year or two. It is not usually necessary to repeat this mopping more than annually. Whenever this mopping is done, it must always follow a through physical and spiritual cleansing to obtain the best effect.

Add one or two Indigo Blue Balls, and one cup of household Ammonia to two or three gallons of clear water.

The mixture should be used to mop lightly over the

floors of the living space with a damp mop. Please note that the floors must be physically cleaned first, or you will just be mopping this solution over dirt. Since making the dirt stronger is not really what you are trying to do, it is necessary that the home be thoroughly physically cleaned before strengthening the place with this mopping.

Moving Into Your New Quarters

Now that your home has been physically and spiritually cleaned, it is time to start moving in your things. First, move in a small table. With you and those whom you will be living with gathered around the table, you should communally share a slice of bread between all of you. Once you have shared your first food in the new apartment, you should pray the sixty third psalm together. You may then pray together that your time in the new quarters be one of happiness and joy. This being accomplished, your home is now ready for you to move in your furniture and other things. You may now fully occupy it as your new residence.

Using Cinnamon In The Home

Real estate agents recommend that anyone showing a home that is for sale bake bread in it, so that those viewing the home feel that it has a warmer and homier atmosphere. Another way to obtain this warm and homier atmosphere, particularly of you do not wish to either sell your home, or bake bread, is to put a calming and domestic vibration into the home. This may be easily accomplished by adding a teaspoon or two of cinnamon to a cup or two of boiling water. Let the water continue to boil in an uncovered pot, preferably an iron pot, adding more water when necessary. Allow the steaming cinnamon odor to permeate throughout the house. By adding more water when necessary to the vigorously boiling cinnamon water in the pot, you will soon have the cinnamon odor making its way all through your home. Cinnamon adds a very calming and domestic odor, and a similar warm and friendly vibration, to any residence. This is something that is actually quite beneficial for anyone to do in his or her home or apartment from time to time. I thoroughly recommend doing this frequently. Boiling cinnamon water just after the new moon, every month is particularly beneficial in keeping a warm and comfortable domestic feeling in your living quarters. This also maintains a general feeling of peace and calm in the home. This practice is particularly recommended for homes where there are young children, as it is both protective and calming for them.

Protection Of A Home

The most effective simple protection of a home is to wash the floors with ammonia water on a regular basis, say at least once a week. Any excess water can be poured down the steps of the entryway, if you live in a house. In an apartment, washing the floors, especially entryway with ammonia water is quite effective as well.

A tea made of a teaspoon of powdered clove placed in a cup of boiling water, and allowed to reach room temperature, may be used to coat the clean walls of an entryway, or the clean inside of the front door and its doorframe. The outside of the door and the doorframe may be washed with ammonia in the wash water, to remove any negativity found there. However, only the inside of the front door and its doorframe should be washed with the clove tea.

The use of clove tea at least annually provides an effective barrier against all kinds of minor negativity, including negativity that might be sent against anyone who is living in the house. It is also surprisingly effective against both those who send malochia against the home, or those who try to send any other kind of directed negativity to the occupants. The clove washing does not usually need to be repeated very often, but repeating it every three months or so may be advisable, especially if you live in what is usually known as a bad neighborhood. More frequent repetitions of the clove wash are useful if you know that you have several enemies who might wish to harm you.

Door Charms And Spells

There are a variety of charms and spells that may be placed on doors or put near or around the doorway to the home. A few of the most common and easily prepared charms are given below. A spiritual practitioner usually prepares the most frequently used of these, the sword of St Michael, for their clients. However, if you would like to make one for your home yourself, there is no reason that you cannot do so. Here is how the best of these rather common but quite useful domestic charms are made.

The Sword Of St. Michael Spell

Obtain a small toy sword, or at least a small model of one. The sword should not be over six inches long, and can be as small as an inch or so in size. The only important thing is that it is what you personally consider to be a good representation of a sword, and that it should be made of metal. Many religious and spiritual supply stores sell these swords, pre marked as St. Michael's sword. This is a common and frequently used protection spell for both homes and apartments.

First, locate a place for the sword, just inside your front door, and on the open side, not the hinge side. Wash this spot thoroughly and place a small picture hanger there, one that you can use to hang the sword. Usually there is a small loop or something on the purchased sword with which to hang it. If not, you must now tie a white thread tightly around the sword, so that it may be suspended from the picture hanger. The best place to hang the sword is at about eye level, either on the doorframe or on the wall next to the open side of the door. Please note that this charm must be placed opposite the hinge side of the door.

Once you have the sword ready to hang, you are ready to prepare it for its task. Begin by washing the sword you are going to use thoroughly in cold running water. Then, holding the sword in your hand, pray to St. Michael the Archangel, or to the deity of war in any other pantheon you may prefer. In your prayer, ask that the saint or deity symbolized by the sword become the protection of your home, holding it safe from any evil influence that may be sent against it, emanating from any source whatsoever. As soon as the prayer is finished, hang the sword at the place you have prepared for it next to the doorway.

The Hunters Arrow Spell

A sharp pointed hunting arrow, similar to the arrows used in hunting deer, may also be hung near the doorway for the same purpose. Do not use one of the blunt target arrows used in most archery sets. The arrow must be sharp, one that is able to bring down game. The necessity of using a sharp hunting arrow makes this charm dangerous to put in place in a home that has small children living in it. The use of this protection is recommended only in those homes where there are no children under eighteen, and where the danger of having a sharp arrow placed by the doorway can be respected buy the occupants and visitors.

The arrow is usually prayed over in the name of St. Sebastian the martyr, or another of the many Roman soldiers who were martyred for being Christians in the early years of the church. It may also be prayed over in the name of either the warrior or the hunting deity of any other pantheon you may prefer. If you wish, you may pray over it to St. Melvin, as he is the Patron Saint of the Infantry. The infantry ultimately is the best protector of the homes and people of a nation.

The Crossed Key Charm

One or two keys of the old fashioned kind used as pass keys, often sold in pairs in hardware stores, may be hung by the doorway with the prayer that the door be opened to health, love, prosperity, and opportunity, and locked tight against illness, negativity, or any kind of evil. If two keys are used, they should be crossed, and tied together where they cross with white thread. The keys may be hung either above the center of the doorway, or to the open side of the door. If they are hung at the open side of the door they should be hung above the sword of St. Michael, close to the top of the door.

The Coco Butter Cross

Once you have a clean door on the inside of your house, and have washed it with the clove protection solution and allowed it to dry, you should make an equal limbed cross on the inside of the door with coco butter. This is done to protect the home against any negative influences. While the coco butter cross, which should be placed at or above eye level, does not replace the clove wash, it is of great assistance in the overall protection of the home.

Negative non-physical forces can see this cross through the door, and they tend to avoid homes so protected. Those humans who are traveling, usually unconsciously, in their non-physical or astral body during the night also avoid passing through these marked doors. This is a strong protection for the door of any living quarters. This coco butter cross may be used on the inside of bedroom doors as well, where the cross will also discourage non-physical adventurers.

Should you or someone in your home be having unusually detailed or odd sexual dreams almost every night, you may wish to place a coco butter cross on the bedroom door. These dreams are infrequently caused by the obsessive thoughts of someone else, and while this is not a very common difficulty, the precaution is simple enough. Should the dreams stop once the coco butter cross has been placed, these obsessive thoughts were probably the cause.

You can buy coco butter in sticks at almost all drug stores, as it is frequently used as a skin treatment.

A Door Charm Against Sickness

When you believe that you have been plagued with illness in your home, the following door charm has been used as a method of asking the universe for assistance in their healing. This would be when there are two or more members of the family who are ill, or when someone in the house has been ill for more than a week. This charm is not a treatment for any physical condition. Its purpose is only to provide a means of notifying the universe that you have had more than your share of illness, and you don't want or need any more sickness in your home.

Tie a purple ribbon around an ear of Indian corn, where the shuck or outer covering joins the ear. Now attach the ear of corn behind the entrance door of your home or apartment. The Indian corn and the purple ribbon are a notice to the universe that you no longer need any more sickness or illness in your home.

Some people prepare this charm every fall, when the Indian corn is frequently sold as a Halloween decoration. They then replace the charm the following fall. If you like to have a decorated doorway, this is a more useful decoration to have than most others.

Removing Negativity From A Sleeping Person

When a person is sleeping in your guest room, and you wish to remove any negativity or harmful thoughts they may be having, placing a single white rose in a small vase will usually have this effect. Place the rose in the room before you show them to the guest room, and do not make any big issue about it. When there are many negative thoughts around the person, the rose may wilt, or even turn black overnight. In this case, it should be put into the garbage in the morning, and replaced with another white rose. The rose should be placed where it is higher than the head of the sleeper, and ideally near the head of the bed. However, there are no real restrictions on this, so anywhere in the bedroom is usually satisfactory. Its purpose is only to clear up negative thoughts. Should you wish to protect yourself from their thoughts, in addition to sleeping with night water, you might place a white rose in your own bedroom as well.

I have recommended this technique be used when relatives come to call, or stay overnight. Especially when the persons they are visiting, has what are politely known as 'issues' with the visiting relative. This is a generally successful way of protecting yourself, as well as assisting in healing any breaches you may have with the visiting relative. I am always reminded in this regard that we chose our friends, but that God chooses our relatives for us, usually to teach us something.

Making Spirit Traps

If you feel threatened by negative influences of any kind, you should first take the time to look into yourself and try to learn why you feel this way. If you believe that you may have some reason to fear influence from any of these negative entities, there is a very old, and a very strong protection that you may use to counteract them. It is known as the spirit bottle, or sometimes known as the witch's bottle. One of the many versions of this spell is given below.

Take a small bottle, such as a baby food jar, and place a dozen or more pins, needles, and pieces of broken glass into it. Now add about a teaspoon of black ink. Fill the bottle with water, and place the lid tightly on it. Put this bottle on the windowsill of your bedroom. It is very discouraging to any non-physical entities that might try and enter your bedroom at night.

Another astral snare or witch's bottle is made in much the same way using a more volatile liquid, such as rubbing alcohol. Otherwise, it is made the same way the previous witch's bottle was made. Adding the volatile liquid makes the effect of the bottle somewhat stronger, and it gives it a slightly poisoning effect toward spirits and any other roaming astral entities that may try to pass through the opening that it protects.

You should also be sleeping with a glass of water set out in your bedroom as well. Place a full glass of water out by the head of your bed before you go to sleep. Empty the glass in the morning, using the hand that you do not write with. Then rinse the glass out three times and set it aside, dedicating it to be used only for this purpose. See my book, '*Spiritual Cleansing*' pages 27 and 28 for more information concerning this kind of protection at night. In my opinion, this is one protection that everyone should use every night. It solves an amazing number of problems with both night visitors and turbulent or uncomfortable sleep.

If you have been using water in your bedroom while you are sleeping and are still having bad or turbulent dreams, you should add a small piece of camphor to the water when you set it out each night. A piece the size of the head of a kitchen match will be quite enough.

A glass of water may be placed by the front door of the home for this purpose as well. It will adsorb at least some of the negativity brought in by visitors, as well as by family members returning home. This glass should be emptied out at night, the glass rinsed, and refilled. It should be placed at the door overnight, to discourage night visitors. This glass should also be dedicated to the purpose of protecting the home. Changing the water morning and night will insure that it provides protection to the home and those who live there.

If there is a particular person that you wish to keep out of your quarters, a similar spell will do this for you. Prepare a small bottle with pins, needles, nails, and broken glass. Write the name of the person you wish to keep out using a lead pencil, writing the name on a piece of scrap paper. Put the paper with the person's name on it in the bottle. Now fill the bottle with water and about a teaspoon full of black ink. Close the bottle tightly, and place it upside down by the front door to your home.

A Simple General Purpose House Cleaning

To clean out simple negative vibrations from a home, apartment, or other or living space, buy a head of lettuce that is fairly firm and hard. Starting in your living quarters at the furthest point from the front door, roll the head of lettuce through the house, kicking it gently with your left foot. When a leaf breaks off, pick it up and put it in a trash bag. Kick the lettuce all through your house until you come to the front door. Then kick it out the door, or carry it with your left hand and put it into the garbage. This cleansing may be done as often as you believe that you need to do it. If you wish, you may perform this cleansing every week. It is rarely ever necessary to do this more frequently, even when you feel that you may be under serious psychic attack.

Removing The Stain Of Death

When someone has died in a house or apartment it is often difficult to remove the heavy emotion laden thought form that the deceased has left behind them. This thought form often causes members of the family to dream vividly of the departed person. In a home where someone unknown to the family has died, the same effect may be felt, with the new occupants of the home or apartment having vivid dreams of the person who has perished. Naturally, this can be quite disturbing to the peace and tranquility of the household.

A mixture of a cup each of ammonia and seawater, with about two tablespoons of Florida Water, (a commercial cologne), added to the mixture can be used to mop up and permanently remove such a heavy thought form of death. It may be necessary to mop the area where the person died more than once. Mopping the area, such as the floor of the bedroom, twice a day for three consecutive days will remove the heaviest and most insidious thought forms of the departed. This will even remove the last thoughts of fright, pain, and panic, which were formed in the mind of those who have been murdered.

Those who have died peacefully in bed should have their mattresses sprinkled with the solution given above on three consecutive days. The room in which they died should be thoroughly mopped at least once each day on three consecutive days. Once the mopping has been done, pleasant smelling incense should be burned in the room. For this purpose, I recommend burning frankincense on charcoal.

Protection When Under Psychic Attack

Despite the interesting plots found on television, in books, and in the movies, there is only rarely any really serious influence directed to other people by magicians working against them. For one thing, it is a lot of work to direct non-physical forces magically to influence another person. Any magician, whether working for good or evil, has to have a very good reason to be willing to put the time and effort necessary into influencing another person psychically. In most cases, it is just not worthwhile for the magician to take the time to do so. Even the most evil magician would get nothing out of the other person by using psychic influence that they could not get from that person, or from someone else, with much less work and effort.

Verbal persuasion, or salesmanship, is usually the most effective magical technique available to us all. Most people are far more open to the suggestibility of ordinary salesmanship than they can ever admit to themselves that they are. Almost all human beings are both suggestible and easily convinced by an emotional or heart rendering appeal. That being the case, the use of magic is a waste of effort when words can be so effectively used by someone wishing to influence another to do as they desire.

So-called magical wars, conflicts between magicians, are usually over very quickly. The stronger magician either completely ignores the other one, and the weaker magician's work falls back on them, or the stronger magician strikes back swiftly and swats the weaker one as if he was an annoying mosquito. In either case, the magical war is soon finished. Such wars are nothing for the average person to ever be concerned about, as they will never be involved in one. In fact, very few real magicians are ever involved in any kind of magical war either. Truly powerful magicians recognize each other at sight, whether physically or non physically. Unless they have a serious ego problem, they tend to stay away from the territory, and the people, claimed by other magicians.

On the other hand, perfectly ordinary people can often become emotionally obsessive about someone else. Their strong emotion driven obsessive thoughts, constantly dwelling on the object of their desire, can often cause the person they are thinking about to have uncomfortable dreams, and may even cause them to have very disturbing nightmares. Fortunately, there is a very simple solution to this not infrequent difficulty.

Placing an egg in each corner of the bedroom will help a great deal in eliminating this problem. To return the negativity being sent to the sleeper, all the person who feels they are under attack has to do is leave the eggs in place for between three days and a week. At the end of that time, break the eggs on the corners of their city block, or on the corners of their property, should they live in the suburbs or the country. Which egg is broken on which corner is unimportant in performing this very effective but quite simple counter spell.

Sealing Doors And Windows

Sealing the doors and windows of your living quarters is something that should be done when you first move into a new home or apartment. The sealing may be repeated at any time thereafter, as it has a beneficial result in the home. The prayer of sealing should be done forcefully, and spoken aloud. The intention of this prayer is to keep out dark and negative forces of all kinds. The prayer below, which is a simple declamation, may be modified as desired by the person performing the ritual. In addition, any powder or oil desired may be used to assist the person in performing this sealing.

Stand before the closed window, doorway, or open passageway. Make an equal limbed cross, from top to bottom, and left to right, while saying:

> "By this sign is this entrance sealed!
> This entrance is henceforth sealed against all undesirable and incognito entities, against all of the hosts of darkness, against all of negative intent, and against all who would hurt or harm. In the name of Almighty God,

the creator and sustainer of the universe."
Amen

Getting Guests To Leave Parties

Another useful spell is one that has been used for many years to subtly tell guests that it's time to leave. This spell involves the use of the household's broom, placing it on the floor in the kitchen with the handle pointed in the general direction of the guests whom you wish to encourage to leave. Through th use of this spell, without saying anything at all to your guests, the guests will usually decide that it is time for them to go home.

An acquaintance of mine turns up the thermostat in his home when he wants his guests to leave. His wife explained that he heard of this technique on a TV science program. Now whenever she feels the temperature in the house rise, she places her broom on the kitchen floor. She assured me that this 'double barrel' technique always empties their house of guests within a half hour.

CHAPTER SIX

Charms And Simple Useful Protections

Many people wear charms, or jewelry that has been designed to avert trouble or protect them from difficulty. There are several theories as to why these charms and jewelry actually work to protect the wearer. I shall mention a few of the several theories that I have encountered over the years, although I have no one favorite theory.

The first and most pragmatic theory states that such charms and protections divert the eye of the beholder from the person, making it difficult for anyone to harm or influence the person wearing the charm through giving them the evil eye. I once had a salesman tell me that he never wore round or oval shaped jewelry, as it drew the eye of the prospect, making it more difficult for him to sell to them. This is certainly an interesting explanation, although I must admit that I cannot credit it with protecting against anything other than malochia.

The second theory states that these charms and pieces of jewelry have an inherent virtue of their own. According to this theory, through the symbolism of the charm and the intent of the person wearing the charm, any negative forces that are sent toward the person are negated and rendered ineffective. This theory is usually applied to such charms as crucifixes, saints' medals, and other religious symbols. I have noticed that for some people, wearing these medals and religious symbols does seem to have a strong protective effect for them.

Another theory states that the effectiveness of any charm or protective amulet is a function of the strength of belief of the person wearing it. If the wearer believes the charm will work for them, it will work for them. This theory seems to me to also be valid, especially in the case of some of the more unusual charms and protections I have seen a few people wearing from time to time. I have seen people wearing monkey's paws, and other odd charms, which I have not been able to connect to any particular system of protection other than the belief of the wearer.

You may take your pick of these theories, but whichever theory you chose, you must accept that the charms worn for psychic protection by many people actually do seem to work quite well for them. That is the most important point for you to consider, as some people wearing charms of various kinds do seem to be immune from even the most vicious kinds of psychic attack.

Among the most common charms people wear, to promote psychic safety is the horn. This is a small gold or silver horn shaped charm favored in Italian communities. Another common charm is the Figa. This is a carved hand with the index and little fingers extended, making the American Signing Language symbol for "I love you." This charm is also favored among Italian and southern French people, but it is found in Greece as well.

In our American melting pot, the use of particular charms is not usually ethnically restricted. A Puerto Rican man in my neighborhood has a large gold crowned red plastic horn suspended from the rear view mirror of his pick up truck. I mentioned to him that it was a favorite Italian charm against the evil eye. He informed me that the charm was also a favorite in Puerto Rico. I have also seen a number of the young people in my neighborhood wearing tattoos of Chinese good luck characters, although none of them are oriental. I suppose this is just the American melting pot at work.

Another highly favored protective charm is the natural shark's tooth, which is often wrapped with a silver wire and suspended from a neck chain worn by both men and women. The cat's eye, a small circular shell that has a natural design like a cats eye in it, is another protective charm worn by many people. This charm is often made into earrings and worn by women who do psychic counseling. I believe that the cats eye charm is protective by its own virtue, as I know of people who have worn it on a necklace concealed under their clothing, and have found it to be very protective for them, even in that concealed location.

In addition to these charms, there are also any number of religious symbols that may be used as charms by those who are believing members of the religion that the charm symbolizes. The Christian cross or crucifix is the most commonly seen of these charms, but the Jewish Star of David is another charm that is often seen. Moslems of both sexes may wear a 'Hand of Fatima' charm on a necklace. All of these charms directly identify and connect the person wearing them to their religious faith, which certainly protects them, at least to the actual strength of their faith in their professed religion.

Other charms seem to have an inherent virtue in themselves. I have seen both Jewish and Muslim men wearing charm cases that apparently had verses of scripture placed in them. In three cases I can easily recall, I was able to see with the non-physical sight that these charm cases actually glowed non-physically. Two of these were on charms being worn by Muslim men, and the third on a charm being worn by a Jewish man dressed in the costume of the orthodox Hassidic Jew. I have no idea what was in these charms, but I found the non-physical glow around these charms to be quite fascinating.

Culture and accepted belief have given certain symbols a power of their own. One example is the pentagram. The five-pointed pentagram star found on our national flag is considered a symbol of good when a single point of the pentagram or star is up. When there are two points up, and the single point is down, the symbol is taken as being one of evil. I personally believe that this identification dates only from the writings of Eliphas Levi, the nineteenth century French author who popularized both black magic and the occult arts with his books. He popularized the 'Goat of the Sabbat,' as a figure that combines both white and black magic. The pentagram and its inverse, with two points up, is popular among some of the many counter culture occult groups today.

On the other hand, the pentagram, although feared by many fundamentalist Christians, and written about as a powerful symbol of the occult, has become an almost universal symbol indicating the desire of the wearer for spiritual evolution. In this sense, it has become as valid a sign of protection as the crucifix, for those who wear it for this purpose.

The small white plastic elephant charms that are frequently seen on necklaces and charm bracelets also supposedly have two meanings in their symbolism. When the elephant has its trunk raised, it is supposed to be a sign of prosperity and spiritual evolution. When the trunk is down, it is supposed to be a negative, even a malign influence. I have no idea how this identification came about, but the Indian elephant God Ganesh, is usually shown with his trunk down, or was shown that way in the few illustrations I have seen of that deity. However, I have always considered Ganesh to be a beneficent deity.

Other charms have other meanings, so you should always investigate the symbolism of any charms that you may decide to wear. This may be done quite effectively at your local public library. Some charms may be attractive, but have meanings quite contrary to your actual intentions, or your real desires in life.

I recall a young lady who came to me complaining that her birth control never seemed to work, regardless of what means she used to insure that she not become pregnant. I noticed that she was wearing an African fertility charm on a leather thong around her neck. A man she had dated several years previously had given it to her as a good luck charm just before they amicably separated. I asked her if she had found that she easily became pregnant shortly after she began wearing the charm. She admitted that had been the case. A month or so after she stopped wearing the charm, her birth control method began working correctly for her once again.

A Sexual Charm

The arrowhead, either made of real flint or of metal, is indicative of the hunter, and thus is often worn by those who are looking for, or hunting, for something. At one time, this was a charm worn by many men who spent their time in the singles bars of New York. I even had a young man bring his newly purchased silver arrowhead necklace to me to bless so that he might be successful in meeting compliant young ladies. It certainly made an interesting sexual attractant spell for him.

A Waist Cord

I have found one concealed charm uniformly effective for those who use it. This is a cord worn around the waist. The cord may be as small as a piece of package twine, or as large in diameter as a piece of clothesline. It should be about a foot or so longer than the waist measurement of the person wearing it. Tying the cord around your waist, usually with a square knot, with the intent of sealing yourself off from negative forces will accomplish that result for you quite well. I have never heard any complaints about this charm, so I recommend it to you for your daily use.

The Water Of Life

Not quite a charm, but a useful annual practice, is to bath or wash yourself in wine once a year. This need not be an extensive wash, as all that is required is to stand in the tub or shower and pour a bottle of wine over your head, allowing it to run down your body, going where it will.

This action provides refreshment for your non-physical body, and is often quite beneficial to the person who does it. The wine wash has a different effect than the beer bath, which has been mentioned previously as a means of removing malochia. In ancient times, alcohol was called the Water of Life or Aqua Vita. Wine was used in bathing and in body rinses, as regular scented alcohols are sometimes used today. I believe that this is because the non-physical refreshing effects of this wine wash or wine bath were well known to the ancients.

A client of mine who is a student of the classics told me that the ancient Romans used to bathe in a mixture of water and wine, considering it beneficial to their health. She admitted to me that she treats herself to a bath in champagne on her birthday every year, using two bottles of champagne to a tub of water. She told me that she believes that this is both refreshing to her, and a way to get her new year off to a good start.

If you have difficulty with alcohol, or if you are allergic to drinking an alcoholic beverage, you should not use either this wash or bath. On the other hand, if you have no difficulty with alcohol, you might find that taking a bath or 'washing with wine' to be refreshing to your sprits from time to time.

CHAPTER SEVEN

Miscellaneous Useful Spells
Two Spells For Women

Removing Tangles From The Hair

All women who have long hair (Christian women were directed to keep their hair long by St. Paul, who said it was given them for a covering.) will appreciate this spell. Brushing or combing through tangled hair can be quite painful, and may even be destructive of the hair. Many women have used this simple spell to successfully comb or brush their hair free of snarls and tangles.

The woman herself, or any other person who is brushing the woman's hair, should pray this spell while they are brushing or combing the woman's hair.

"Mary the hairdresser who anointed our Lord with Holy Spikenard to her everlasting glory, I beg and beseech you to free (me) or

(this good woman _named here_) of the tangles which are in her hair, and to restore her whole to her former pure and loving state."
Amen.

For A Painful Menses

Praying for relief from a painful menses over a yellow or gold colored ribbon, and then tying the ribbon around the waist has proven to be effective for many women. The yellow ribbon may be set aside for that purpose, and used whenever required by any of the women in the household.

Generally Useful Spells
A Garlic Good Luck Spell

Garlic has many uses in magic, as well as in healing. One of the more interesting uses of a garlic bulb is this good luck spell, which I learned from an old Italian woman who once lived in my apartment building. Visiting her in her apartment one day, I saw this charm hanging in her window. I asked her about it, and after we had become better acquainted, she told me how she had made the charm. A few days later, I made one and hung it in my own window. I was quite pleased with the result. Over the years, I have made a number of these charms for clients. They all seem to like this charm as well. This is a general good luck charm, not one that will act to bring any specific thing into the life. It does seem to increase the general luck of the owner however, and due to its construction, it adds a pleasant but subtle perfume to the room.

Take a whole fresh garlic bulb, and stick nine straight pins into it, around the circumference of the bulb. Place a brass tack in the bottom end, and a steel nail into the top end. Tie a white thread to the nail, so that it may be suspended. Now wind a white thread around each of the pins in succession, weaving the thread, passing it over one pin and under another. You will end up with a white thread ringing the garlic bulb. The garlic is then to be soaked in a perfume or cologne of your choice overnight. The completed charm is hung in a window, where the sunlight may reach it. The garlic charm should be dipped in perfume or cologne at least once a week thereafter. When troubles threaten, or your luck seems to slacken, you may dip the garlic charm into the perfume as often as once each day. It is not necessary to soak the charm overnight ever again.

Divination With The Bible

An interesting Amish man showed this rather different divination method to me. I had my doubts about it, so he took his well-worn bible and an old-fashioned iron key and proceeded to demonstrate to me just how well it worked. I was amazed by the simplicity of this method. I soon found that there were several other versions of this method. I shall give the spell, and then the two most popular variations of it I have learned.

A key is inserted in a bible, and the bible held closed, either by tying it with a string, or by placing three rubber bands around it, as the Amish man did. The bible is suspended, by holding the key in the hand. When a question is asked, the bible will jump or move when the answer is spoken.

As an example of the kind of question that may be asked: "Which crop will fetch the highest price at harvest? Corn, Soybeans, Wheat, or Hay?" The bible visibly jumped when soybeans were mentioned.

The variations of this spell I have found all seem to relate to the preferred location of the key in the bible. The two most popular locations are the first pages of the Gospel of John and in the book of Ruth, where the words spoken by Ruth, "Your Gods shall be my gods." are located. I have found that this spell works quite well when the key is located at either place.

Improving Communications in the Home

When communication in the home are difficult, for whatever reason, burning Jasmine scented incense with a prayer that there be better communications between the members of the family is often effective in allowing the members of the family to speak more freely to each other. Air elementals, which are the non-physical force behind all communications, are lightened, refreshed, and made happier, by the scent of jasmine. This allows the communications between people to open up, and encourages people to communicate with each other more freely.

Boiling cinnamon, as was mentioned previously is also helpful in this case, as is burning cinnamon on charcoal. The fumes of cinnamon tend to lighten tensions in the home a bit, which is always a good thing to do. As previously mentioned, I recommend that this be done frequently as a general preventative of problems in the home. The fumes of cinnamon are always protective of family life in general.

On the other hand, you will find that if you lighten up the general vibration of your home first, it will often improve communications in the family as well. One of the best ways to do this is to use an incense that will eliminate the heavy thought forms of depression, discouragement, and despair that often linger in a home, especially during and after any kind of family crisis. If there has been a tense situation in the home, or some recent argument, this treatment may be necessary before attempting to lighten the feeling of the home.

Releasing Heavy or Depressing Thoughts

If you, or another member of your family, has been under stress, or if either of you have been carrying a heavy mental burden, the following incense should be used before an attempt is made to use the jasmine incense to increase the general flow of conversation in the family. You might also consider giving your home a general spiritual house cleaning on a regular basis, something that is always a good idea. If you do a regular spiritual cleansing of your home, using this incense in the family room, kitchen, and wherever your family usually congregates and communicates with each other should be made a regular part of the spiritual house cleaning.

Take equal parts of ground coffee, powdered garlic, and brown sugar. Mix them well and burn some on charcoal, burning about a quarter teaspoon at a time. Allow the fumes from this incense to go all around the home. It is often a good idea to burn this incense in all of the rooms of the house to rid the home of the heavy vibrations of worry, concern, and depression which come upon all of us from time to time.

This incense is particularly good to burn in the bedrooms of teenagers who are passing through late puberty. It helps them rid their surroundings of the heavy and depressing thoughts that so often accompany the physical and mental changes that occur in their life at this time. Following this incense with jasmine incense will often even allow them to talk openly to their family about what is really troubling them.

Clearing the Vibration of a Room

Once the heavy thoughts have been removed and the home has been spiritually cleaned, placing a dozen white flowers, usually white carnations, in the room will assist in keeping the room clear of negativity for a while longer.

The presence of flowers in a room also seem to make the room feel a bit brighter, something which is always to be desired. I believe this is a good reason for keeping flowers in the sick room, especially when there is sickness in the home. The presence of flowers always seems to cheer up the person who is ill, which promotes a quicker recovery for them. A dozen white carnations are usually the best flowers for this purpose.

Avoiding Malochia or Negativity from Others

Malochia or the evil eye is an involuntary condition in which negative energies are transmitted from the eyes of a jealous, greedy, or possessive observer to a usually unknowing victim. While malochia is a condition that causes much physical illness and pain in the world, it is not one that is recognized medically. Malochia may be identified by a metallic taste in the mouth, as well as by sudden stiffness or pain in the spinal column, usually in the back of the neck, but sometimes found in the small of the back.

There is a simple way to make it less likely that you will receive malochia from those people who tend to pass it around like sugar candy to those whom they feel envious or jealous of. Whenever you look at anyone, when you would ordinarily be looking him or her in the eye, instead look at the bridge of his or her nose. Once you have mastered the art of always looking at the bridge of a person's nose rather than their eyes, you will find that you will receive a great deal less negativity from others. Mastering this simple technique will make usually your life much easier and less difficult. People cannot tell that you are not looking them in the eye when you look at them in this way. In fact, they will believe that you are actually maintaining eye contact with them. It is almost impossible for anyone to tell if another person is looking you straight in the eye, or at the bridge of your nose. Those people who can actually tell the difference are not going to be the ones giving you malochia anyway.

Clearing the Head

Sometimes we feel overloaded with thoughts, things to do, and our other daily concerns. When we feel this way we may seek to find a way to 'clear our head' of all of these overly stressful concerns and plaguing thoughts. Fortunately, there is a reasonably simple way for us to do this. It involves using the adsorbing properties of both eggs and water. Take a whole egg, and write your name on it with a soft lead pencil. Place the egg into a clear glass filled with tap water. Now pass the glass around your head three times, moving from your forehead to the left and around the back to your forehead each time.

Next, put the glass of water up high, above your head when you walk around the room, in your house for seven days. Ideally, you should put the glass with the egg in it up high in your bedroom. Unlike the usual practice when you put out night water to protect you as you sleep, in this case you should leave the glass full of water in place for seven days. At the end of seven days, dump the water and the egg into the toilet and flush it all away. Rinse out the glass you used for this purpose with a little ammonia before you wash it and use it for drinking from again.

Another simple remedy for clearing the head of spiritual afflictions involves using the great power of flowers to adsorb non-physical negativity. Place the heads of three chrysanthemum flowers in a bowl or basin of water. Then, standing nude in the tub or shower while holding the bowl, pray for relief from the affliction that you feel around yourself. On finishing the prayer, pour the water of the bowl or basin over your head, allowing the flowers to fall where they may. Now pray a prayer of thanksgiving that the affliction has been lifted off you. This simple wash will remove many ordinary psychic afflictions, as well as most thoughts of negativity and depression that have been sent to you knowingly or unknowingly by other people.

Concern About Spiritual Afflictions

If you are concerned about spiritual afflictions of any kind, I suggest that you purchase a copy of my book '*Spiritual Cleansing.*' It has a great deal of information in it about keeping yourself and your living quarters clear and clean of any negative non physical influences. You may notice that I have cited it several times in this book. I cite it because it has been helpful to a great many people. I sincerely believe that reading it may be helpful to you as well.

Other Books by Draja Mickaharic

Samuel Weiser, Inc. of York Beach Maine originally published my previous books. They are now being published by Red Wheel / Weiser, 368 Congress St. Boston, MA 02210

Spiritual Cleansing—A handbook of psychic protection, first published in 1982.
A Century of Spells—A collection of over a hundred useful spells, first published in 1988.
Practice of Magic—An introductory guide to the Art of Magic. First published in 1995.

These books are all sold on the Internet at Amazon.com
Xlibris is publishing several of my newer books. They are located at: 36 Walnut Street 11th floor, Philadelphia, PA 19106 Or on the Internet, at: *www./Xlibris.com*

Magic Simplified—A series of practical exercises for developing the prospective magician. Xlibris published this book in June 2002
Magical Techniques—A description and explanation of a number of useful but lesser known magical processes. Xlibris published this book in July of 2002

Mental Influence—Magical techniques for influencing other people. Xlibris will publish this book in December of 2002.

These books are available from either: *www./Xlibris.com* or from *www./Amazon.com*

Made in the USA
San Bernardino, CA
08 April 2014